"With her caring s
Dr. Jeanne delivers
to inspire African A
care for ourselves wh.. .... .
lenging lives. As she sees us and leads us, Dr. Jeanne leaves us with
a bounty of spiritual and practical hope and help for our caregiving
seasons. It's a beautiful gift for others, but first to ourselves."
—**Patricia Raybon**, *Our Daily Bread* contributing writer and
award-winning author of the Annalee Spain Mysteries

"Dr. Jeanne Porter King's newest book, *Caring Well*, is a vital
source of encouragement and wisdom for caregivers. Her ability to
weave personal caregiving stories with Scripture provides space for
Dr. Jeanne and God to walk with us on the caregiver journey. The
90-day devotional gives us practical ways to prioritize the care of
our mind, body, spirit, and soul; overcome the guilt of self-care; and
accentuate our well-being as we care for others."
—**Dr. Antoinette G. Alvarado**, CEO of Targeted Living
Coaching & Consulting, LLC and founder of Harmonize Your
Life Women's Self-Care Network

"*Caring Well* is not only a compassionate guide for those navigating
the demands of caregiving but also a profound spiritual companion. As a caregiver for my mom, I found solace and strength in its
pages. . . . The book's core message—that through faith and the em-
bracing of one's spiritual resources, one can find the strength and grace
to navigate caregiving—is both empowering and transformative."
—**Sheila Agnew McCoy**, fitness and aging lifestyle coach,
author, and speaker

"Dr. Jeanne Porter King is bold enough to speak some unspoken
truths about caregiving that caregivers dare not utter. She provides
caregivers the tools to get beyond those crucible moments and provides the means to forge an enlightened path toward seeing the
gift, the blessing, and perhaps the joy in the testing of the spirit that
comes with choosing to give of self to another."
—**Patricia Jones Blessman, PhD**, licensed clinical psychologist

"As a caregiver, retreat consultant, pastor, daughter, aunt, and friend
wearing many hats, I found this book not only life-giving but an
opportunity to care for myself. Each devotion, each story, each

Scripture, each reflection anchored me and allowed me to inventory my life, giving me an opportunity to exhale and remember who I am apart from the roles and responsibilities I have."
—**Dr. Julie Welborn**, associate pastor of LaSalle Street Church and owner of Perfect Peace Consulting, LLC

"*Caring Well* is a masterpiece providing devotions that address caregiving from multiple perspectives. Jeanne addresses burnout, caregiving fatigue, and the grieving process of caring for the person who initially cared for you. Caregiving can often feel very lonely but *Caring Well* showed me that I am not alone on this journey and provided me with Scripture and tools to guide me along the way. I highly recommend this devotional."
—**Pamela Dykes, PhD**, communication professor, professional coach, and author

"A delightful guide, provoking reflection for those of us who desire to stay strengthened in our caregiving journey. The book exonerates caregivers who feel guilty for the challenges they face and offers devotional encouragement and hope."
—**Sanreka Watley**, aka Phoebe London, author of *Sam and Uncle Joe: Learning to Serve and Protect*

"*Caring Well* offers a transparent, candid account of the highs and lows of caregiving as well as wise, godly guidance on how to manage your emotional, mental, spiritual, and physical well-being during the caregiving journey. Reading the devotions makes you feel like you're in a support group led by an affirming coach. I wish I had a book like this when I was caring for my grandmother."
—**Yolanda Y. Harris**, former caregiver for her grandmother

"*Caring Well* . . . addresses cultural attributes of African American Christians who are tending to their loved ones. It centers caregiving as a calling, with a need for those on the frontline to make *caring for themselves* a spiritual practice. Challenging, real, heartwarming, and nuanced, each devotion is designed for reflection—encouraging an intentional path of self-care and well-being. Regardless of where you are on this God-driven journey, this book is a valuable tool."
—**Claudette Roper**, interdisciplinary artist & media consultant, and adjunct professor, Columbia College Chicago

CARING WELL

90 SELF-CARE DEVOTIONS
for the African American Caregiver

JEANNE PORTER KING

VOICES | Our Daily Bread Publishing.

Caring Well: 90 Self-Care Devotions for the African American Caregiver
© 2024 by Jeanne Porter King

Author is represented by the literary agency of Embolden Media Group, Lake Mary, Florida, emboldenmediagroup.com.

Requests for permission to quote from this book should be directed to: Permissions Department, Our Daily Bread Publishing, PO Box 3566, Grand Rapids, MI 49501; or contact us by email at permissionsdept@odb.org.

Bible permissions statements can be found on page 227.

Interior design by Michael J. Williams

ISBN: 978-1-64070-334-6

Library of Congress Cataloging-in-Publication Data Available

Printed in the United States of America
24 25 26 27 28 29 30 31 / 8 7 6 5 4 3 2 1

Mom, it was my privilege to be your caregiver. I am thankful for the legacy of care you passed on to me, and that I now pass on to others.

CONTENTS

Section 3: Personal Well-Being 59

Section 4: Relational Well-Being 81

Section 5: Mental and Intellectual Well-Being 103

Section 6: Emotional Well-Being 125

Section 7: Physical Well-Being 147

Section 8: Vocational Well-Being 169

Section 9: Environmental Well-Being   191

INTRODUCTION

Caring for others is what we do as Black Christian women. In addition to working in or running businesses, leading ministries at church, and serving in our communities, we routinely choose to care for loved ones in need.

You may provide care for an elderly mother, as I did, or for an aging father, as my good friend Pam is. You may care for a special-needs child or an adult child whose capacity to care for themselves has diminished. Or perhaps you're caring for a spouse, an ailing sibling, or a good friend. Our care is an act of love. I refer to the people we provide care to as our loved ones throughout the book.

Your caregiving may require around-the-clock care or only part-time care. It may entail providing support for elderly relatives who want to continue living on their own but need daily assistance.

Caregiving can be an exhausting, draining emotional journey. It can be one of the toughest things you will ever do—as well as one of the most rewarding.

While you care for your loved one, you also must take care of yourself. I know that sounds challenging right now, especially if you are in the early stages of caregiving. But keep reading; I will provide many self-care ideas in this book that are helpful and edifying.

As caregivers, we want to provide the best care possible for our loved ones. And as African American caregivers, our culture expects us to care well—that is, effectively and sacrificially— for our loved ones in need. But to do so, caregivers must *be* well—in spirit, soul, and body.

I've written this devotional book primarily for African American women of faith, as caregiving for others is a core value of women in our culture. We are expected to take care of others within our families and communities. Yet I know men and women of all races who provide care for loved ones. No matter what your circumstances, as a caregiver, you will benefit from this book as you learn to navigate between your caregiving role and taking care of yourself. Sometimes it seems that no one really prepares any of us, regardless of our background, for the challenges that come with caregiving. And if you are like me, you don't want to sound like you're complaining as you describe the realities of caregiving: disrupted schedules, the unpredictable needs of your loved ones, and sleepless nights. These wear on you emotionally, mentally, physically, and spiritually. So, each of us must be intentional about caring well—that is, we must tend to our own well-being while caring for others.

As caregivers of faith, we can draw upon Scripture and prayer to help sustain us in our caregiving. In fact, our faith also can help fuel the self-care we need to take good care of ourselves as we care for others.

This devotional, comprised of ninety readings, will help you take care of yourself while caring for others. I address wellness and self-care in three areas: soul, mind, and body. These wellness components are interrelated and together address the whole you. That's right, Scripture can provide encouragement and inspiration around your total being!

Each entry begins with a Scripture. Our faith is fueled through the Word of God and the promises found therein. Each devotion has a short reflection story to connect with you. Sometimes I share a story from my own caregiving journey to remind you that you are not alone. At other times I share a general thought from Scripture to encourage you to keep on keeping on. Each entry includes a prayer that you can use. I close each devotion with a reflection that encourages you to write whatever is on your heart, ideally at the end of your day. Consider keeping a journal to record your reflections.

Because I found caregiving to be unpredictable, these ninety devotions can help you develop a routine for your own care. Too often our day gets consumed with such things as meal prep, feeding, organizing medicines, assisting with grooming, and coordinating doctors' and nurses' visits. Even with caregiving assistance, it can become all-consuming.

So, whether first thing in the morning with your tea or protein smoothie, late at night after you've put your loved one to bed, or during a bathroom break (let's keep it real), pull out this devotional and spend some time caring for *you* by connecting with the Word.

Remember that while you care for others, God cares for you. Yes, you. May this devotional guide remind you of just how very much you are loved and cared for by God, and help you normalize a routine of caring for yourself.

 Scan this code to view a personal message from the author, Jeanne Porter King.

SECTION 1

ENHANCING SPIRITUAL WELL-BEING

1

THE SPIRITUAL LIFE

Abide in Me, and I in you. As the branch
cannot bear fruit of itself, unless it abides
in the vine, neither can you, unless you
abide in Me. —John 15:4 NKJV

Our spiritual well-being is vital to caring well.

Jesus used the metaphor of a grapevine and its branches
to teach His disciples about the spiritual life. In this imagery,
God our heavenly Father is the vinedresser, Jesus is the vine,
and we are branches of this vine. The Spirit flows through the
vine out to the branches, and we remain spiritually vibrant as
we abide in the vine.

Jesus continues on in this teaching to stress that believers
cannot bear fruit unless we abide in the vine and stay connected
to Him. This connection enables us to bear much fruit. We
connect closely to Christ, we abide in Him, through an awareness of God's love, praying, meditating on the Word, reading
God-honoring books and materials, worship, and other spiritual practices.

There is another crucial process related to fruit-bearing
to consider—pruning. Vinedressers or gardeners periodically
must prune back the dead leaves and stems of grapevines so
that the life sap within each vine can flow out to the healthy
branches, nourishing the fruit waiting to come forth.

For many of us, caregiving can feel like we are going through
a pruning process. In some ways, we are. God uses the experiences and challenges of caregiving to prune away the tendencies

in us that are not fruitful. By abiding in Christ, the life-giving Spirit flows through us to produce "this kind of fruit in our lives: love, joy, peace, patience, kindness, goodness, faithfulness, gentleness, and self-control" (Galatians 5:22–23 NLT).

There are times when caregiving circumstances test our spirituality. We may respond to our loved one with an impatient tone or speak harshly to a healthcare professional. We must repent as the Spirit reveals to us the cause of those actions and attitudes. There will come a time when we will ask God to prune those tendencies from our lives and give us the grace to change.

The more intentional we are in cultivating and developing our spiritual well-being, the more helpful it will be to care from a spiritually healthy place. The key to cultivating our spiritual vitality is by abiding in Christ.

Dear God, the gardener of my soul, thank you for placing me in the vine. Allow the Holy Spirit to tend to the soil of my heart to keep me loving, joyful, peaceful, patient, kind, good, gentle, and self-controlled in my caregiving. And when I am not, give me the grace to repent and self-correct quickly. In Jesus's name, amen.

Reflection: Think about your day and examine when you feel you were fruitful and when you were not. Note any patterns that emerge upon reflection.

2

GOD'S GRACE IS SUFFICIENT

And He said to me, "My grace is sufficient
for you, for My strength is made perfect in
weakness." Therefore most gladly I will rather
boast in my infirmities, that the power of Christ
may rest upon me. —2 Corinthians 12:9 NKJV

During a busy season for my company that could have buried me, I learned a crucial caregiving lesson that freed me.
I had worked my business's schedule around my mother's caregiving needs. Between our home caregivers and me, we kept a
schedule for my mother that created familiar routines for her,
but often disrupted mine.

I shared with my prayer partner, "Please keep me in prayer,
as this is a particularly challenging season with my business. I
have several deliverables for the next six weeks and feel a bit
stretched." I wasn't on top of the projects as I typically am.
They were getting done, but it was taking longer. I felt I was
not operating in my usual strong-Black-woman mode.

The truth is, I didn't feel as much in control as I like to be.
And needing to be in control was my weakness. I would never
be totally in control of anything, and I needed the grace of the
One who *is* in control.

Grace is God's presence in our everyday lives that fills the
gaps. And we will always have gaps in what we can do on our
own. Grace is the outpouring of God's love into our lives,

filling our hearts with the assurance that we are not on this journey by ourselves. Grace is the flow of God's influence in and around us, assuring us that Christ's power abides with us and rests upon us. Grace floods our lives with what we need when we need it.

Grace settles our anxious thoughts and calms our fears. Grace covers us. God's grace saves us, and it also sustains us. It keeps us sane and safe.

As a caregiver, perhaps you have a thorny situation that you want God to atttend to so you can be stronger in handling your business. You may want more time in the day. Perhaps you want your loved one to be less dependent upon you. Maybe you want other family members to be less demanding. Or more present. Whatever your situation, know that God's grace is "more than enough—always available" for you (2 Corinthians 12:9 AMP). God's grace works best in our weaknesses. It is in our weaknesses that perhaps we can receive God's grace most fully.

You may not want to brag about your weaknesses as a caregiver. Still, you can find joy in knowing that God is present with you, even when you feel the weakest.

Thank you, God, for your grace. I rejoice that you are present with me at this moment, ready to fill in the gap. I surrender to your grace. In Jesus's name, amen.

Reflection: In what ways did you see God's grace show up for you today?

3

TAKE HEART

I have told you these things, so that in
me you may have peace. In this world you
will have trouble. But take heart! I have
overcome the world. —John 16:33

Understandably, caregivers can become overwhelmed by
the weight of caring. Whether it is caring for an elderly
parent, a special-needs child, or the issues in one's neighborhood, attending to the concerns and needs of others can be
overwhelming. We can feel agitation in our spirit and suc-
cumb to worry and frustration, perhaps because we feel out
of control and at a loss for what to do. Our hearts can grow
heavy and troubled.

At such times we must remind ourselves of Jesus's promise
to His disciples when He was about to face the most overwhelming situation of His earthly life: the cross.

Jesus reminded His disciples that "in this world you will
have trouble" (John 16:33). Think about that; the One who
carried the cares of His disciples and was about to carry the
world's sins to the cross acknowledged the troubling weight
of caring. He knew we would face difficulties and that these
trying circumstances would threaten to overcome us. Yet He
tells us to take heart.

In biblical language, the heart is seen as the seat of our emotions and will. It sometimes is interchanged with the word *soul*.
The heart is the core of our being. Troubling situations can
threaten to cause us to lose heart and hope.

Jesus's command is assuring. He says, "Take heart! I have overcome the world" (John 16:33).

Take heart means to be encouraged or to have confidence in something. Facing His impending death, Jesus took the time to help His disciples make sense of what was happening around them and to them. He declares to them that no matter what difficulties they faced, He has achieved victory over their troubling circumstances. He will do the same for you and me.

So how do we "take heart"? We remind ourselves of what the Lord promised us, even commanded us to do. Though troubling situations press in on us, our circumstances will never press Christ from our hearts. We can have peace by knowing that no matter how out of control our world feels, our Lord is still in control.

We can take heart because Christ resides in our hearts.

Dear God, I thank you that I can take heart. The enemy cannot and will not steal the joy and peace from my heart. In Jesus's name, amen.

Reflection: Today, focus on one promise found in God's Word that speaks to your caregiving circumstances and can help you "take heart."

4

LISTEN FOR THE STILL SMALL VOICE

Then He said, "Go out, and stand on the
mountain before the LORD." And behold, the
LORD passed by, and a great and strong wind
tore into the mountains and broke the rocks
in pieces before the LORD, but the LORD
was not in the wind; and after the wind an
earthquake, but the LORD was not in the
earthquake; and after the earthquake a fire, but
the LORD was not in the fire; and after the fire
a still small voice. —1 Kings 19:11–12 NKJV

The part of caregiving that was the hardest for me was
handling Mom's health issues. I'm not trained as a nurse
or medical doctor, and her flare-ups and health crises were
downright scary. I didn't always know what to do. You probably can relate.

One morning was particularly challenging, as I couldn't
seem to get her breathing stabilized, even after a couple of
breathing treatments. I was at a loss for what to do. I went
to a quiet place and plopped down. I encouraged myself, "It's
going to be all right."

And then, deep within my spirit, I heard, "And you don't
have to be the one to make it all right."

That gentle whisper inside my spirit brought a sense of
relief and a release. As my fear subsided and was replaced by

the belief that this situation would turn out all right, I texted Mom's nurse practitioner for a consult. I did not have to figure this out alone.

We caregivers too often feel pressured to make everything "be all right," as if we control every situation. Sometimes that pressure comes in the form of the noisy voices of others; other times it is from self-inflicted chatter. We are tempted to play the role of superwoman, trying to fix everything that ails our loved one, and then find ourselves drained from overworking and over-fixing.

We find someone in Scripture who experienced the highs and lows of trying to make everything all right. Elijah ran for his life, after which God took Elijah to a place where God could give Elijah instructions for the next step of his journey. As we read in the Scripture above, God whispered, and Elijah heard the voice of God.

When you are at a loss for what to do, find a place where you can hear what is necessary for the next step. You must calm your frightened thoughts and emotions and pray for wisdom and help. Then listen for the still, small voice of the Holy Spirit. Learn to discern the gentle whispers of the Spirit from the loud, distracting voices of guilt, pressure, and pride.

Dear God, who whispers softly but surely, I yearn to hear your voice guiding me and giving me peace and direction. In Jesus's name, amen.

Reflection: What do you need to do today to become quiet and still so you can hear the gentle whisper of the Spirit, which can provide you with just what you need? Somewhere on your long to-do list, carve out some time today to listen to that still, small voice.

5

YOU'RE INVITED

Then Jesus said, "Come to me, all of you who
are weary and carry heavy burdens, and I
will give you rest." —Matthew 11:28 NLT

I received a call from one of my closest friends. She heard
something in my voice and asked how I was doing. I replied
honestly, "Brenda, I'm weary." Brenda is a strong preacher who
boldly uses her voice to proclaim the gospel of Jesus Christ.
Yet this usually strong-voiced woman's tender reply oozed
through the phone line and into my heart. "Oh, Jeanne, I hear
that." After listening some more, she prayed for me.

Weariness is more profound than physical tiredness. It occurs when our souls are tired. It's fatigue of the heart, in which
our energy drains and we have no idea where we'll get more
strength.

Jesus beckons for all who are weary to come to Him. He
invites all of us who work so hard, feeling fatigued under the
weight of our labor, to take his yoke and learn from Him.
There, He promises we will find rest for our souls.

I had to tell the truth in coming to Jesus that day and beyond. And let me be clear: my mother was never a burden to
me. She brought joy into our home. But caregiving can be
burdensome. And in our communities, we don't often feel safe
enough to voice the truth about this labor of love.

In coming to Jesus, the Lord taught me to care more wisely.
I exchanged my yoke for His. A yoke is a beam that links the
collars of two oxen together. When plowing a field, the yoke

25

keeps the oxen on pace with each other and allows each to share the load. For Jesus, His yoke symbolizes that we are to be so closely connected to Him that He paces us and helps carry the burden. We can then carry out our tasks and responsibilities from a position of trust, relying upon the gifts and graces given to us by the One to whom we are yoked.

Too often we take on caregiving as a burden, not a blessing. The burden I felt early on transformed into a blessing as my life and priorities changed. The load grew lighter as the Lord directed me in how to give up and let go of lower-priority items on my schedule.

You will be no good to yourself or your loved one if you try to care from a place of weariness. The Lord invites you to connect with Him in order to lighten your load.

Dear God, I need to be so connected to you that my load becomes lighter. Thank you for the invitation, and by your grace, I humbly accept. Please show me the way. In Jesus's name, amen.

Reflection: Spend time in prayer, asking God to identify His yoke or means of connecting you with Jesus to lighten your caregiving load. What is the Lord inviting you to off-load or reprioritize?

6

SING A NEW SONG

He has given me a new song to sing, a hymn
of praise to our God. Many will see what
he has done and be amazed. They will put
their trust in the LORD. —Psalm 40:3 NLT

During the pandemic, my husband, mother, and I gathered for a nine p.m. prayer every evening to close our day. It started as a prayer ritual for my husband and me at the beginning of the COVID-19 shutdown, and when Mom came to live with us, she joined us every night.

We started off our time of prayer with a praise or worship song. We all had favorite praise and worship artists, and each night we took turns asking Alexa to play a song to start our prayer time.

One of the biggest delights of that time of caring for mom was singing new songs that we'd discover. These new songs expanded our repertoire of praise music. Singing these new songs to the Lord brought joy to our hearts and connected the three of us.

In at least five places in Scripture, the psalmist or prophet encourages the people to sing a new song to the Lord. One psalmist testified that the Lord heard the people's cries and delivered them from a horrible situation (Psalm 40:1–3). Another declared God's glory and thanked Him for victory and the manifestation of God's righteousness (Psalm 96:1–3). A couple of psalmists admonished the people to sing new songs praising God's salvation (Psalms 98:1; 149:1). In another place, God had promised to send a suffering servant or messiah to bring forth justice. The prophet declared that good news warranted singing a new song (Isaiah 42:10).

Singing new songs of praise demonstrates the power of praising God. Singing lifts our spirits as we sing about God's marvelous works. Singing songs that declare God's goodness reminds us of the greatness of God in our present circumstances.

Sometimes old songs remind us of God's past activity in our lives; it is good to reflect on and be reminded of what God has done. But singing new praise songs is an opportunity to recognize what God is doing right now. New songs often bring a fresh perspective on a characteristic of God and enable us to see with new eyes what God is doing in our midst.

Singing a new song can help open your heart to the joy of caregiving because God is helping you and your loved one along the way.

Dear Lord, thank you for putting a new song in my heart. I am grateful that you are faithful and a constant source of joy and delight. In Jesus's name, amen.

Reflection: Take a moment to explore a few new praise and worship songs that speak to you about the goodness of God in this present season.

7

NEVER TOO BUSY TO PRAY

Pray without ceasing.
—1 Thessalonians 5:17 NKJV

Too often, we caregivers don't carve out time to pray. We may get out of the habit of praying regularly because of the increased needs of the one we care for. We feel too busy to pray. However, as the older saints of my faith tradition used to say, "If you are too busy to *pray*, then you are *too* busy!"

Even within our busy caregiving lives, we must develop a practice of prayer. Developing a practice of prayer means making prayer a habit—not in the superficial sense of checking the box that we said a prayer today. Making prayer a habit instills the discipline to always pray without ceasing.

Here are some tips I found helpful in developing and maintaining a habit of prayer during caregiving.

Set a regular time and place to pray. Just as we have our loved one on a schedule, we must develop a plan that includes our prayer time. To do this, we may need to get up earlier than the rest of the family and spend time in the morning praying, to set the tone for our day. We can also set the end of the day as the time for prayer.

Develop a structure for praying. We can start with some deep breathing to settle into our time with God and invite the Holy Spirit to hover and breathe fresh upon and through us. From there, we can spend some time worshiping God. Worship helps to set our mind godward. Worship helps settle us into the presence of God, not asking anything but positioning ourselves to listen and hear in the Spirit.

Seek the Lord. Of course, in our prayer time we are invited to seek the Lord for solutions and strategies to the issues of our lives. And it is in seeking that we also can pray on behalf of others.

We can then close with celebration and praise.

Keep a prayer journal, writing out your requests. Note what you hear from the Lord in your time of prayer. And as you pray for others, note how the Lord answers. Reviewing your prayer journal can encourage your heart to see how God has worked on your behalf, and it documents your progress in spiritual growth.

Praying is power for all of us, but especially for caregivers. Praying enables us to commune with the Lord and to build ourselves up in the faith we need for the caregiving journey (see Jude 20).

Lord, you hear and answer my prayers. Thank you for the privilege of communing with you. I know that you listen to me. In Jesus's name, amen.

Reflection: Take stock of your daily schedule. Develop your structure for prayer. If you already have a prayer structure, review it and assess what's working and what's not working. Then determine where you need to tweak it.

8

THE MODEL PRAYER
(PART 1)

"Pray like this." —Matthew 6:9 NLT

In the previous devotion, I invited you to incorporate a daily habit of praying into your busy caregiving life. Today I want to provide a model for prayer that can guide your praying.

But before I do, let me give you a few points of encouragement. Please do not condemn or beat yourself up if you don't follow your prayer schedule perfectly. Life happens with caregivers, and unexpected issues crop up almost daily. If you miss a day, pick up your praying the next day. If you set aside thirty minutes but can only find time to pray for fifteen minutes on some days, celebrate spending those fifteen minutes with the Lord.

Jesus taught His disciples to pray using a model or framework that still works. We call this prayer the Lord's Prayer, probably the most well-known prayer from the Bible.

Different Bible versions show Jesus teaching the disciples to pray "in this manner" (NKJV), to "pray like this" (NLT), or to pray "this way" (NET).

Reverend Suzette Caldwell, author of *Praying to Change Your Life: A Guide to Productive Prayer*, gives several reasons why we should use the Lord's Prayer as our prayer model, including:

- Jesus said it. It's encouraging to follow the teachings of Jesus. We can have confidence in what our Lord has given us as His disciples.
- The model prayer is God-centered. In this prayer, we pray Godward. We center our trust, requests, and expectations on God, not ourselves.
- The model prayer is strategic. It provides a "balanced strategy for praying."
- The model prayer is transformational. It teaches us to pray for God's will. This prayer aligns our will with God's will.[1]

I have used this prayer as a model for years but found it particularly helpful during my caregiving season.

Sometimes our minds can become so filled with the caregiving issues of the day that we feel scattered when we start praying. The model Jesus gave enables us to focus and pray more targeted prayers.

We all can use a boost to our praying, especially as caregivers. You may have asked others for more effective prayer strategies. Thankfully, the Lord anticipated our need—just as He did for His first followers—and has given us a model to follow.

Lord, you hear our prayers. Thank you for being in the details of our lives and providing us a model for praying that will help us focus when we are with you. In Jesus's name, amen.

Reflection: Take a moment to think about your current pattern of praying. What's your strategy? How effective is it? Consider how you may want your prayer life to grow, especially while you are in this season of life.

9

THE MODEL PRAYER (PART 2)

"Pray like this." —Matthew 6:9 NLT

Models are created to provide a framework, so we don't have to do the work of inventing something new. Remember the old saying, "There's no need to reinvent the wheel"? The thought behind the statement is that someone has already created the wheel, so we can use their wheel and expend our energy and time on other things.

That's how I see the model prayer. Yesterday we looked at some of the advantages of using this approach to prayer. Today we will explore the six parts of this prayer, using pastor Suzette Caldwell's teaching in her book, *Praying to Change Your Life*. Each line of the prayer will be explored. Think of this as a guidepost to helping us navigate through our prayer time. We don't need to repeat these exact words as if by rote. Instead, Jesus's words provide the topics for our prayer. We can add content that fits our own lives.

1. Worship: "*Our Father in heaven, hallowed be Your name*" (Matthew 6:9 NKJV). Jesus taught us to start by acknowledging God, calling God "Father," and reverencing God's name. This first part helps us to *home in on* the One to whom we are praying and to stay mindful of God's greatness and sovereignty. This part of the

prayer focuses on worshiping and praising God with adoration and reverence.

2. God's Will: *"Your kingdom come. Your will be done on earth as it is in heaven"* (Matthew 6:10 NKJV). Here the Lord teaches us to align our will with God's will. When we pray for God's will, we anchor our praying.

3. Our Needs: *"Give us this day our daily bread"* (v. 11 NKJV). Here the Lord references our daily needs. We can articulate our needs and the needs of *others*.

4. Forgiveness: *"And forgive us our debts, as we forgive our debtors"* (v. 12 NKJV). Here we ask for forgiveness. And we must keep our hearts open and be mindful that God calls us to forgive others as well.

5. Protection: *"And do not lead us into temptation, but deliver us from the evil one"* (v. 13 NKJV). This is our opportunity to ask for protection from temptations and evil.

6. Praise: *"For Yours is the kingdom and the power and the glory forever. Amen"* (v. 13 NKJV). We close with praise just as we opened our prayer with worship, like bookends on a shelf.[2]

Prayer is a journey into the spiritual realm, and what is known as the Lord's Prayer in Matthew 6 guides that journey.

God, you who hears and answers prayers, thank you for providing a model that guides me in communing with you. In Jesus's name, amen.

Reflection: Use this model as you pray today. In your journal, note what it was like for you to pray this way.

10

BLESSED TO BE
A BLESSING

*All praise to God, the Father of our Lord Jesus
Christ, who has blessed us with every spiritual
blessing in the heavenly realms because we are
united with Christ. —Ephesians 1:3 NLT*

To bless someone is to speak well of them. God blesses us by speaking His favor and love upon us. Too many people associate God's blessings only with material things. In their estimation, people are blessed because they have wealth and status, drive a nice car, or live in luxury.

According to Ephesians 1:3, God has blessed us with *spiritual* blessings. In other words, God pronounces blessings upon us from His heavenly storehouse. The term *heavenly realm* refers to the place where God dwells and Christ is exalted. It reminds us, as believers, that we exist in two realms. The earthly realm is the material world that we physically live in, and wherein we see, touch, taste, hear, and smell with our five senses. Yet because we are "in Christ," we also coexist, or walk by faith, in the spiritual realm. Ephesians 2:6 tells us we are seated with Christ in the heavenly realm. These spiritual blessings shape our character, order our relationships, and enable us to live purposefully.

Spiritual blessings are all the divine gifts and privileges we can access because of our union with Christ and His Spirit. We read in Ephesians 1:4–8 that these blessings include, but are not limited to, our being chosen, adopted, redeemed, and forgiven.

Privileges come with being God's adopted ones. For instance, our worship and prayer enable us to spend time in God's presence, where the Spirit produces fruit: love, joy, peace, patience, kindness, goodness, faithfulness, gentleness, and self-control (Galatians 5:22–23). We likewise bless our loved ones as they experience the Spirit's fruit when they interact with us. We are forgiven, and we, likewise, forgive. We are given access to the Spirit's wisdom, so we act wisely.

The real blessing for us, especially in this season of caregiving, is that God has given us the needed spiritual resources to live out our lives and fulfill our tasks and assignments.

That is the core of caregiving: blessing our loved ones through the blessings bestowed upon us. We choose to love the ones we care for because God has chosen to love us and has given us the capacity to choose love over hurt or resentment.

We are blessed so that we might be a blessing to others.

Dear God of all spiritual blessings, thank you for bestowing blessings upon me so that I may share these blessings with the ones I love. In Jesus's name, amen.

Reflection: Think of the spiritual blessings mentioned above. Which ones were you particularly aware of experiencing and sharing today? How might you become more aware of sharing these spiritual blessings with others?

SECTION 2

DRAWING FROM THE CULTURE

11

IT TAKES A VILLAGE

At last the wall was completed to half its height
around the entire city, for the people had worked
with enthusiasm. —Nehemiah 4:6 NLT

Caring for loved ones is an expectation for many people in Black communities. We hail from a people who took into their homes people displaced by slavery's cruel and capricious practices. From these displaced people, our forebears united and created family.

Though caregiving patterns are changing, many Black caregivers draw strength and support from family members, extended family, friendship networks, and members of our churches. An African proverb states that it takes a village to raise a child; I believe it also takes a village for caregiving.

Village-keeping and collaborating aren't new. They were even practiced in Nehemiah's time, when it took the village to secure the walls of Jerusalem. The walls had been destroyed by war and needed to be rebuilt. Nehemiah took a leave of absence from his job and traveled with supplies to Jerusalem, where he led the charge to restore the wall. Nehemiah couldn't do the work alone; he persuaded community members to come together and repair the walls. The work was burdensome and expensive. But the people had a mind to work together to show their love and care for their community's safety.

Caregivers in Black families may experience similar circumstances. Most will need to continue working full-time, although some will leave their jobs or take a leave of absence.

The financial demands of caregiving can be significant, and sometimes building and maintaining a supportive network can feel heavy.

According to the American Association of Retired Persons (AARP), "African Americans often have more burdensome caregiving situations than their non-Hispanic white or Asian caregiver counterparts. They also tend to be younger, are often unmarried, have poorer health, and frequently have to balance caregiving with full-time jobs."[1] Yet other studies show there is an "expectation among African Americans that family and community members will look out for one another and [these caregivers have a] relatively greater commitment to religious practices and values" that reinforce a caregiving ethic.[2]

In our communities, caregivers often feel a sense of purpose and a calling to care for our loved ones. And many Black caregivers see their current caregiving as a means of giving back to family members who cared for them, and helping family members in need maintain a level of "independence and higher quality of life."[3]

Over the next nine days, we explore the cultural dimension of caregiving as exhibited through multigenerational caregiving and cultural values of care transmitted through songs and stories.

God, you call us to build people up. Help me with
my caregiving journey, and help me identify my
loved one's care needs. In Jesus's name, amen.

Reflection: Develop a list of people in your immediate and extended family, and your friendship or church network, whom you may call upon for assistance.

12

THE GOD OF OUR ANCESTORS

May the LORD our God be with us as he was
with our ancestors. —1 Kings 8:57 NLT

Not long ago, I received a direct message (DM) on Instagram from a young man in Cleveland, Ohio, asking if we were related. With his inquiry, he included a picture of what turned out to be my maternal great-grandmother, great-grandfather, and great-uncle.

I recognized a name my mother often spoke of: Grandma Cal. But I had never seen her face. I came to learn that when Grandma Cal (who was my mother's paternal grandmother) got up in age, she relocated from the family homestead in Tennessee to Columbus, Ohio, to live with her daughter Ida, and close to her other daughter, Christel. Years later, when my mother's mother (I called her Granny) suffered a cerebral hemorrhage, she came to live with my mother, father, brother, my baby sister, and me. I was eleven years old but remember those years of pitching in to help Mom care for Granny. I draw strength from this lineage of godly women who cared for their mothers as they aged or became less able to care for themselves because of illness. I draw strength from the God of my maternal ancestors, who gave them strength to care.

While dedicating the temple that he built, King Solomon recalled his lineage and the God of his ancestors. For Solomon, the desire to build a temple to worship God was a value passed on from his father, who worshiped God through songs, psalms, and poems.

Caring for our loved ones is one of our cultural values. Cultural values help people maintain their identity, survive, and thrive in their environment. Sometimes the environment in which we live as Black people can be hostile.

Yet we are not alone. We can draw strength from, remember, and reflect on the God-given power of our ancestors who knew beyond a shadow of a doubt that God would take care of them.

In many cases, we hail from the lineages of caregiving ancestors. For some of us, it may not be people in our immediate family but our extended cultural family. Somewhere down the line, we have the testimonies of ancestors from our culture who cared for loved ones or fellow community members because of the bond of love that connects, honors, and reverences our humanity.

God of our ancestors, who sustained our people in dangerous times and enabled our ancestors to demonstrate your love in their acts of care, I pray this day for strength that will sustain me as I care for my loved one. In Jesus's name, amen.

Reflection: Reflect on the following words extracted from the Black National Anthem:

> Yet with a steady beat,
> Have not our weary feet
> Come to the place for which our [ancestors]
>   sighed?[4]

What do these words mean for you on this day as a caregiver?

13

THE LEGACY OF CARE

One generation shall praise Your works
to another, and shall declare Your
mighty acts. —Psalm 145:4 NKJV

Though you will not find the word *legacy* in Scripture, the concept and practice of legacy are solidly fixed in the Bible in the stories of one generation passing on the mighty works of God to the next.

Likewise, understanding the legacy of care can be restorative for caregivers. In the intimate time of caring for loved ones, we hear stories of God's working in the past, and our caregiving, in turn, results in stories of God's work that will be handed down to future generations of caregivers.

You see, the origin of *legacy* arose from the sending of ambassadors or envoys. The word stems from the Latin *legare*, which means to "send with a commission, appoint as deputy, appoint by a last will."[5] It was about sending a representative to share the desires of another.

In that sense, the legacy of care is about how each of us serves as a representative of God, sharing the love of God with one in need.

We caregivers inherit values from our ancestors and transmit them to the next generation through our care stories. A legacy of care is about the multigenerational stories of caring for one another—through times of both challenges and blessings. The legacy of care is about the stories passed on to us. We continue to pass on the stories of the power of God to sustain us in caregiving when we keep the grand scheme of things in mind.

I remember one time in particular during my mother's ninety-first birthday weekend. My sister and her four children came to town to spend the weekend with Mom, my husband, and me. We sat in Mom's room, talked, and listened to her recount stories from her past.

Mom strolled down memory lane, and hearing her stories brought joy to our hearts. We captured several of her stories on video, using my cellphone. One of the last things she said that evening was that she wanted all of us "to love one another and to love the Lord." What an incredible testimony and legacy of love for us to inherit from Mom and to pass on. I still smile when I watch that recording.

The legacy of care is not about perfect daily actions but is about our presence to love another, whether a family member or friend. It's about passing on the mighty works of God through our love and compassion.

Dear God, help me care with legacy in mind, to have something to pass on to the next generation as a witness to your faithfulness in caring for my loved one and me. In Jesus's name, amen.

Reflection: What is an incident from today that bears witness to the mighty works of God in your life as a caregiver? Write it out and be prepared to share it as the Holy Spirit leads.

14

THE FAITH OF OUR MOTHERS

I remember your genuine faith, for you share the faith that first filled your grandmother Lois and your mother, Eunice. And I know that same faith continues strong in you. —2 Timothy 1:5 NLT

In the last devotional entry, I wrote about the legacy of care passed down from my mother, grandmother, and great-grandmother. You may have a similar lineage or family tree line centered around care.

From what I know about our culture, the legacy of care is passed down from our mothers and is anchored in faith.

Paul, in writing to his mentee, Timothy, commends him for his genuine faith. Timothy did not cultivate his faith in a vacuum or on his own. His mother, Eunice, and his grandmother Lois nurtured his faith.

Rarely are women named in the Bible. Yet for the Bible to commend both of Timothy's maternal ancestors for nurturing an authentic faith in him is striking.

Many of us hail from women who were strong Black women, who cared for others often at the expense of caring for themselves. The stereotypical superwoman persona will not help us as caregivers today. Being everything to everyone will burn us out. Yet there is another side of our mothers' strength that we must embrace. The memories and images of faith-filled women who prayed and sang their way through caring will help us as caregivers. Whether it was mother, grandmother, godmother, or neighborhood mothers down the street or in the church, we share the faith that filled these women with the commitment, courage, and compassion to care for others.

It took faith and trust in God to express their love for caring for their loved ones. They have passed that down to us.

These women trusted God to be a present help in difficulty. They trusted God to send physical support through siblings, nieces, neighbors, and church members to help when they had to go to work or grocery shopping. They trusted God to keep their loved ones safe when they had to accompany them to the hospital by ambulance or place them in care facilities.

Our ancestors trusted God to help them keep on keeping on when they may have felt like giving up. These caring women trusted God, knowing that when they had done all they knew to do, they could commend their loved ones into the hands of a loving God.

Today we can draw strength as we recall the faith of our mothers that was shared with us and anchors us now.

Dear God, it takes faith to care. Thank you for strengthening my faith as I provide care. And thank you for reminding me that I hail from a community of women who model caring. In Jesus's name, amen.

Reflection: Recall a woman from your family, church, or neighborhood who took care of others. How did she live out her faith in caring in a way that did not wear her down?

 Scan this code to view a personal message about this devotion from the author, Jeanne Porter King.

15

KNOW THAT YOU KNOW

And we know that God causes everything
to work together for the good of those who
love God and are called according to his
purpose for them. —Romans 8:28 NLT

My Granny used to tell us we've got to "know that we
know." As a praying woman of God, a Black church
matriarch, she wanted her grandchildren to know deep down
inside of God's assurance in our lives.

Granny's knowing was a deep knowing that resided in our
minds and the depths of our hearts. It is that profound sense
of knowing that prompted songs of faith in God such as "You
Can't Make Me Doubt Him."[6]

The knowing my Granny spoke and sang about wasn't
knowledge that comes from a book. It was a deep-seated
knowing that grew from an intimate relationship and experience with God.

In the biblical sense, to know means "to be aware, consider
or perceive."[7] In both the Hebrew Bible (or Old Testament)
and the New Testament, this knowledge comes from experiencing the thing one knows about. In the New Testament,
this knowing extends to our experience of God through Jesus
Christ.

The way the older folks of my faith tradition put it when
going through a trying time, "If God did it before, God can
do it again!" In other words, their experience with God keeping them in the past was evidence of the faithfulness of God

in the present. Their experience with God led them to declare that God wouldn't stop being faithful now.

In fact, they hung their confidence in God being faithful to them on the promise that God causes everything to work together for our good. They knew that the trying situation might not feel good and that it may not even look good. But they knew in their hearts that God would work it together for their good according to His will.

Be encouraged, caregiver. Know that what God has done for others, God can do for you. I'm a witness. Know that God has been faithful, brought you to this point, and is getting you through this season of your life. Know that God is working it all together for your good.

Today, declare that you know that you know that God is with you.

Dear Lord, thank you for the reminder that I know you have my caregiving situation in your hands. I thank you for the promise that you will cause even this to work together for my good, and I will be able to let others know that I know God is faithful! In Jesus's name, amen.

Reflection: What did you come to know about God today?

16

CARING IN THE LIGHT OF GOD

This is the message we heard from Jesus and now
declare to you: God is light. —1 John 1:5 NLT

Light represents many things in Scripture, most revealing as
a character description of God. Light is an energy source.
When applied to God, He is our dependable energy source.
The light shines in the darkness; in God's case, nothing can
extinguish the light. No matter how dark the days and nights
might seem, we can count on God to enlighten our minds.
Light serves as a guide, especially in dark places. As our light,
God guides and illuminates our paths.

Light, in Scripture, also stands for truth. We know God
is the ultimate truth, and because of His faithfulness, we can
trust the integrity of God—what God promised in the Word,
we can hold on to.

And it is in the challenging times of caregiving that the
Zulu hymn "Siyahamba"[8] comes to mind. The tune is catchy
and stays with me. You can hum and sing it through the day,
and I am a witness that it will lift your spirits. If you are un-
familiar with it, google it and find a rendition of this song. As
uplifting as the tune, the words are even more encouraging,
full of determination that we can and will move forward because of our God's light that envelops us. We march forward
in God's light.

When I've heard this song in churches, the worship leader

adapted and exchanged the lyrics with "We are walking in the light of God. We are dancing in the light of God. We are living in the light of God."

Yes, the truth is that no matter how oppressive forces try to stop us and hold us back, we can be sure that we can move forward empowered and guided by the light of God. This song fuels our faith to persist in the light of God being with us.

There will be times in your caregiving experience when you may feel overwhelmed and overpowered by the dark forces of bad news, unexpected flair-ups, and adverse reports. Still, by God's grace-filled light, you can move forward in your care.

You, too, can adopt and adapt this song's lyrics, making a personal declaration: *I am caring in the light of God.* God's light is your source of energy for the caregiving task. God's light is the source of wisdom you'll need to think through caregiving challenges and seek consultation to make enlightened decisions.

The darkest day will never extinguish God's light. Look to the light and march forward.

Dear God of light, I receive your strength even now.
Please give me the energy to care for my loved one and the
enlightenment to choose wisely. In Jesus's name, amen.

Reflection: Spend some time reflecting on the qualities of light and how God has shown those characteristics to you.

17

LIFT OUR VOICES AND SING

Around midnight Paul and Silas were praying
and singing hymns to God. —Acts 16:25 NLT

We hail from and are a people who, though imprisoned
by slavery, segregation, and degradation, sing. We sing
prayer songs, protest songs, praise songs, love songs, and blues
songs.

To sing is to express the soul's joys and sorrows. To sing is
to put to melody the sentiment of the heart. Singing can lift
a downcast spirit. It can unload a burden. Singing can allow
us to wallow in agony one moment and then rise to the cre-
scendo of ecstasy the next.

We are a people who know the power of voice and song. In
our midnight hour, like Paul and Silas, whom the authorities
unjustly imprisoned, we too can sing.

With slavery in the not-too-distant past and on the heels
of a crumbling Reconstruction, James Weldon Johnson captured the promise of singing with "Lift Every Voice and Sing."
Now known as the Black National Anthem, Johnson wrote
this hymn in 1899. His words were put to music by his classi-
cally trained brother and colleague, John Rosamond Johnson.
It was first sung by five hundred Black schoolchildren in 1900
at an assembly to honor the birth of Abraham Lincoln.

The song reverberated in the hearts of those who heard
it and has resounded through the ages to capture the spirit

of struggle and resilience of our people. This song speaks to the range of emotions of our people: from praise to lament to prayer.[9] "Lift Every Voice and Sing" is a song of uplift that captures the existential struggles of a people collectively and each of us individually.

Sometimes we get so caught up in caregiving tasks, though, that we forget to sing. We can lose sight of the songs embedded deep within our spirits—songs of hope, of joy. Songs that uplift and encourage. Sometimes the cacophony of demanding tasks threatens to drown out the songs that lift us up.

Today, let's remember to lift our voices and sing. Lift our voices and sing "a song full of the faith that the dark past has taught us." Lift our voices and sing "a song full of the hope that the present has brought us."

"God of our weary years,"[10] *thank you for bringing me this far on my way. In Jesus's name, amen.*

Reflection: Listen to a recorded version of "Lift Every Voice and Sing." Which parts speak most deeply to where you are in your caregiving journey?

 Scan this code to view a personal message about this devotion from the author, Jeanne Porter King.

18

GOD OF OUR SILENT TEARS

Those who sow in tears shall reap
in joy. —Psalm 126:5 NKJV

When's the last time you had a good cry? Tears are not a
sign of weakness but can be a sign of hope. Tears play
a role in our spiritual health as well as in our physical and
emotional health.

Some tears remove "debris such as smoke and dust from
our eyes," and lubricate "our eyes to help protect them from
infection."[11]

Emotional tears that flow in response to our hurts and pain
"flush stress hormones and other toxins out of our system."
These tears release the "feel-good chemicals" oxytocin and en-
dorphins. These chemicals "ease both physical and emotional
pain."[12] We can feel such relief after a good cry.

Then there are tears that flow in response to God's presence or the hope of God's presence. Though we cry, we trust
God to transform our sorrow into joy.

Those tears are a gift from God to us and also our offering
to God. The nineteenth-century British pastor Charles Spur-
geon called tears liquid prayers and a means of intercession on
behalf of others. These tears flow in hopes of God interven-
ing in our situations.

Such was the expectation of the ancient people of God.
The Israelite nation went through devastating situations time

and time again. They learned to look to God in good times and bad. They weren't perfect, nor are we. But the ancient people of God left us a gift called the Psalter, or the book of Psalms, that chronicles their spiritual journey and their very human interactions with God at all times.

They maintained an expectation that God would move on their behalf. For anyone to go out sowing seeds while they are crying says they trusted God to bring good out of the current dire situation. God saw their tears and heard their cries. We too can hold on to the belief that God will move on our behalf.

The expectation that God will move on our behalf is called hope. We may sometimes be hurt, but we still have the God of hope. As caregivers, the fact that we can cry is a sign that we still have hope. As we hold on to God and open our hearts, tears may flow. Our tears get God's attention (Psalm 56:8).

Of course, the tears that accompany a prolonged sadness are informative for us also. When our crying is constant and we can't bring it under control, we need to seek help from a professional counselor, medical doctor, or spiritual director.

Tears are nothing to be ashamed of. They are signs of our humanity.

"God of our silent tears,"[13] *I know you hear and see me. In Jesus's name, amen.*

Reflection: Pay attention to the situations that trigger your tears. Keep a log in your journal and note your patterns; consider what they may mean for you.

19

BLACK JOY

Count it all joy. —James 1:2 NKJV

As a people, we have experienced untold pain and suffering from the enslavement of our ancestors, to years of segregation, to today's ongoing struggle and calls for equity in healthcare, economics, education, and the like. Yet amidst the challenges our people face, there is a move afloat to remind us of our joy and resilience: The Black Joy movement.

For our community, Black Joy has come to represent a means for "making space for . . . positive experiences apart from and in opposition to the trauma, tragedy, and struggles perpetuated by anti-Black racism "[14] and the constant depictions of Black trauma in media. Those representations often demean our humanity. We, collectively and individually, are more than our struggles.

Writing for the National Museum of African American History & Culture, Elaine Nichols notes, "Black Joy is and has been an effective tool that has allowed individuals and groups to shift the impact of negative narratives . . . in their favor,"[15] and "is and has been an essential act of survival and development"[16] for our communities. Black Joy is a movement of Black people reminding ourselves and others that despite the struggles and assaults on our humanity, we must tell the stories of the joy we experience and express.

Likewise, cultivating such joy is essential for caregivers. Caregiving brings challenges, disappointments, and unexpected changes, sometimes due to the structural inequities our people are subject to. And if we aren't careful while in the caregiving mode, we may focus on the challenges and get mired in the troubles. Yet, as caregivers, we must remember the joy we create through caregiving.

Ms. Nichols says, "Black Joy is finding the positive nourishment within self and others that is a safe and healing place." As caregivers, we have and can find that positivity within ourselves and our community. When faced with trying situations, our faith admonishes us to "count it all joy." That means we are to "consider it an opportunity for great joy" (James 1:2 NLT).

We can assess the situation and look for joy in the situation. We can look around and count the conditions that bring us great joy. No matter how challenging the problem is, we don't have to let it control us. Instead, we control our internal response to the situation, and finding the positive in our situations enhances our well-being.

Dear God of great joy, thank you for reminding me to look around and count the situations that bring me great joy. In Jesus's name, amen.

Reflection: Look around you and count the things in your life that bring you joy, no matter how small. Write them down and enjoy reflecting on them.

20

SELF-CARE AS BLACK RESISTANCE

Remember that you were slaves in Egypt
and that the LORD your God brought you
out of there with a mighty hand and an
outstretched arm. Therefore the LORD
your God has commanded you to observe
the Sabbath day. —Deuteronomy 5:15

In the previous reading, we highlighted Black Joy. Today we focus on Black Resistance. For our people, the two go hand in hand. In the fight for justice and equity, we collectively resist the dehumanizing and stereotyping of our people in collective and everyday individual actions. As caregivers, we can resist the stereotypes of the Black superwoman who cares for everyone except herself by prioritizing self-care.

Hailing from enslaved people objectified for their labor, we often believe that our ancestors passed on the primacy of work over our well-being. And as we see in this passage about the formerly enslaved Hebrews, God reminds them that Sabbath-keeping was an intentional act of resistance against enslavement of any kind. Today, many people practice Sabbath-keeping as a self-care strategy of rest and renewal.

What doesn't often get lifted up in our history are the many acts of resistance against White supremacy that our people demonstrated in caring for themselves and one another. For instance, Professor Stephanie Y. Evans traced the history of self-care and its importance in Black women's lives and uncovered a long history of self-care practices such as yoga by Black women. One of the most notable stories she discovered was that the civil rights activist Rosa Parks had a "four-decades-long yoga practice."[17] Mrs. Parks used yoga to care for herself and to be part of caring for the community she advocated for.

Practicing self-care along with Black Resistance runs deep within the history of the Black community. The Black Panthers, Angela Davis, Audrey Lourde, Dr. King, and Mrs. Coretta Scott King, to name a few, espoused and demonstrated the value of self-care. Whether it was prayer, retreats, meditation, mindfulness, or vacations, these Black icons understood the importance of care for self to recover from the onslaught of White supremacy.

Committing to self-care is an act of resistance against a work culture that demands productivity over people. It is also an act of resistance against our tendencies to push through our limits and ignore our bodies, souls, and spirits beckoning for rest and nurture. We must resist both.

Dear God of love and care, you call us to resist our enslavement to anything that hinders our thriving. Help us commit to intentional self-care and to love ourselves as you love us. In Jesus's name, amen.

Reflection: Take a moment to list your regular self-care practices. What are the things you are resisting as you prioritize care for yourself? How does thinking about self-care in this way help you commit to self-care practices?

SECTION 3

PERSONAL WELL-BEING

21

THE POWER OF I AM

Then Jesus told her, "I AM the
Messiah!" —John 4:26 NLT

When we assume a caregiving role, sometimes the demands of that role cause us to limit our identity to what we do as caregivers. How often have we heard ourselves and others say, "I am a caregiver." As lofty as it is to provide care, we are more than caregivers. In the long run, limiting our core identity to a role is unhealthy for our overall well-being.

When we stock all our identity into a role, our sense of who we are and even our self-worth can be seen as contingent upon what we do. For instance, we may have a strong sense of identity if we perform the role well. But when we make mistakes, we may feel inadequate. When the position changes, what are we left with?

Our true identity can best be expressed by the words *I am*. This phrase describes the present truth of who we are. "I am" is the emphatic form of a linking verb—a verb that links two things together. The most decisive form of that verb was declared by God, as revealed to Moses in the encounter at the burning bush: "I AM WHO I AM" (Exodus 3:14 NKJV).

The gospel of John records Jesus using this same structure to give insight into His identity. The form is a naming convention for capturing the essence of one's identity, not one's role, position, or possessions. In the gospel of John, Jesus revealed His identity as the Messiah to the Samaritan woman at the well, using the phrase "I am He" or "I AM the Messiah!" (John

4:26 NLT). In the gospel of John, Jesus gives seven additional "I am" statements to reveal His divine nature and redemptive mission.

- I am the bread of life (John 6:35 NKJV).
- I am the light of the world (8:12).
- I am the door (10:9 NKJV).
- I am the good shepherd (10:11, 14).
- I am the resurrection and the life (11:25).
- I am the way, the truth, and the life (14:6).
- I am the true vine (15:1).

Authentic identity is about who we are at the very core of our being. It expresses our God-given nature and mission. How we live and what we do should reflect who we are. Knowing who we are is critical to every life endeavor.

Yes, how we care reflects who we are and our character.

We will explore who God says we are in the following nine devotions. Reflecting on these truths helps us maintain a healthy perspective and reminds us that who we are fuels what we do and not the other way around. The readings are written in the first person present, so you may embrace them and make them personal. May we each draw strength from these truths as we fulfill our caregiving roles.

*God, who is I AM, help me to walk in my identity
as I give care. In Jesus's name, amen.*

Reflection: Review the I AM statements of Jesus. What does each say about who Jesus is to you?

22

I AM THE LIGHT

You are the light of the world.
—Matthew 5:14 NLT

In Scripture, light is often contrasted with darkness. In the beginning, into a darkened world empty of life, God spoke, "Let there be light" (Genesis 1:3 NLT). Light appeared.

In the beginning, the gospel writer John shares that the spoken Word was life-giving and was the light of humanity (John 1:1–4). John declares that the Word incarnate was Jesus Christ (v. 14). At the beginning of His ministry, as depicted in Matthew's gospel, Jesus tells His followers that they are the light of the world. In other words, as Jesus was ushering in a new kingdom of love, He declared that those who followed His kingdom principles would be light in dark places.

In this way, Jesus used light to represent believers' transforming influence on our environment. Even more, it is from this light that good deeds shine forth and glorify God. Our light speaks of the penetrating influence for good that we have.

Jesus used two images to depict the light that His followers were to be. One was that of a city nestled atop a hill for all to see. The city was a conglomeration of homes and businesses inhabited by people. Their homes and places of business were lit by candles, which provided light for their daily tasks. We are like that light-filled city set ablaze by Christ for all to see.

The second image spoke to the individual believer. That's you. And me. We are likened to the individual lamps or candles set in that city. Each of us is a light shining in dark places.

As caregivers, you might experience some dark days: long, sleepless nights, disappointing prognoses, and depressing news. As darkness surrounds us, Jesus reminds us that we are light—we are His light as He shines through us.

A core part of our identity is the light of God that resides within our hearts and shines forth in our attitudes, actions, and words. That light can penetrate dark, hopeless situations. As lights, we shine.

No matter how dark the day or night, even the seemingly most insignificant light penetrates the darkness. Turn the lights out in your room. Light a candle. The light penetrates the darkness and enables you to see.

And that's who God has made you and me to be, human candles that shine in a darkened world. The caregiving world can be dismal sometimes, but our light helps brighten the way for others.

Dear God, you've said I am the light, and I thank you for giving me the spiritual energy to shine. In Jesus's name, amen.

Reflection: One way we shine is through our good deeds. What is one good act you did today?

23

I AM THE SALT OF THE EARTH

You are the salt of the earth.
—Matthew 5:13 NLT

Salt gets a lot of bad press, especially in our communities where hypertension runs rampant. We are admonished, rightfully so, to limit our consumption of sodium, the primary ingredient in salt, because of its harmful effects on blood pressure.

Salt, however, has numerous beneficial qualities. For instance, I remember when my mother developed a slight skin infection on one of her fingers. Rather than give her an antibiotic, the doctor instructed us to soak mom's finger in warm salt water daily.

When I had dental surgery, my oral surgeons encouraged me to rinse my mouth multiple times daily with warm salt water. Whether for Mom's infected finger or my inflamed mouth, our doctors explained that salt would help reduce inflammation and facilitate healing.

There are numerous references to the positive qualities of salt in the Bible. Salt was used for preserving, seasoning, and purifying. Jesus had these positive qualities in mind when speaking about the identity of those who would follow Him and embrace the principles of His kingdom.

Using a common natural substance that His listeners would have been quite familiar with, Jesus declares that His followers, citizens of His kingdom, are the salt of the earth. Jesus was letting them know that when they lived according to His kingdom principles, their lives would have a preserving, purifying quality that would influence the people around them.

Jesus says the same thing to you as one of His followers today. His words then are just as relevant to you today. Through Christ, you are a preserver. Though sometimes, as you are entrenched in caregiving tasks, you may not feel like you're making a dent in the ever-growing to-dos on your list, but you are making a difference. You have the potential and capacity to preserve peace in conflictual situations or to add flavor to a potentially distasteful matter. Through Christ, you can add zest to your relationships and fresh perspective to your conversations. When mindful of who and whose you are, like salt, you help facilitate the healing process for those around you with your presence and encouraging words.

That influencing quality is a core part of the character of believers. And it can be most impactful when we remain mindful of who Christ has declared us to be.

Dear God, you have made me to be the salt of the earth. Sometimes I forget, but you have instilled within me a preserving, purifying quality that directly results from my being a Christ-follower. Thank you. In Jesus's name, amen.

Reflection: What small thing did you do today that helped preserve peace or positively flavor a distasteful situation?

24

I AM AN OVERCOMER

You, dear children, are from God and
have overcome them, because the one
who is in you is greater than the one
who is in the world. —1 John 4:4

During the height of the first year of the COVID-19 pandemic, my mother came to live with us on October 15, 2020. In less than three weeks, she was hospitalized. As a new caregiver, I felt deflated and somewhat defeated. After caring for herself for all those years, I couldn't believe Mom had come to live with me and ended up in the hospital.

Mom had a chronic condition that my siblings and I knew nothing about. The ER doctor told us my husband and I had gotten her to the hospital in time, because when they typically saw Mom's condition, the person had already died. This doctor's words sobered us and made us thank God for sparing Mom's life. She went on to live with us for almost two more years.

As a caregiver, you too will experience situations that will leave you feeling deflated and defeated. Remember, those are feelings and are not the core of who you are.

Scripture abounds with references to who we are as overcomers because of Christ.

In Romans 8:37, in response to the rhetorical question of what can separate us from Christ's love, the resounding declaration is that despite troubling, even calamitous circumstances, "overwhelming victory is ours through Christ, who loved us" (NLT). One who has an overwhelming victory is an overcomer.

In 1 John 4:4, believers are reminded of who they are—they are "of God" (NKJV) and have overcome those who would proffer lies and make false claims. Sometimes our thoughts lob accusations against us, causing us to feel defeated by the enormity of the tasks before us. But because we are "of God," we can boldly proclaim that the Greater One lives in us and cements our identity as overcomers.

According to 1 John 5:4, because we are born of God, we overcome the world with all its tests and trials. We need not be overwhelmed by the situations in our world. The key to our overcoming is faith in Christ, who defeated death, hell, and the grave.

Dear caregiver, you will face defeating circumstances but are not defeated. You will feel overwhelmed by caregiving challenges, but you are not overcome. You are an overcomer.

Overwhelming victory belongs to you because of who you are in Christ.

When challenges arise and you hear the taunting voices of guilt or perfectionism labeling you a failure, stir up your faith through the Word of God and declare to yourself and anyone else who needs to hear: I am an overcomer through Christ who loves me.

Dear God, I thank you for overcoming power. I praise you because you have made me an overcomer. In Jesus's name, amen.

Reflection: Take time to read one of the Bible passages mentioned in today's devotion. Memorize it, internalize it, believe it, and confess it.

25

I AM ACCEPTED IN THE BELOVED

To the praise of the glory of His grace,
by which He made us accepted in the
Beloved. —Ephesians 1:6 NKJV

Most people want to be accepted by others for who they are. Being accepted for our true selves means that people see the real us. Being accepted means we don't have to put on a mask or facade to pretend to be something we are not. Being accepted means we don't have to hide parts of ourselves to be acceptable to others.

The stress and loneliness of caregiving can sometimes cause feelings of rejection to surface. We make sacrifices for our loved one that seem to isolate us from others. Our circle of friends dwindles, as we don't have the time to talk and connect with others as we did before. Sometimes we wonder if our friends are avoiding us because all we talk about these days centers around caregiving. Or we must put on a happy face and hide the problematic parts of caregiving, lest others think badly of us.

But don't believe lies of rejection. You are accepted in the One who loves you dearly and has called and equipped you for this caregiving task. To be accepted in the Beloved means that we are graced with and embraced by God's love. We are favored by God, not because of anything we did but because of who God is.

We may encounter people who don't really get us. Some

may not understand our choices to rearrange our lives to care for a family member or friend. But the glorious thing is, we are now accepted in the Beloved and don't need to seek affirmation from people who cannot or will not affirm us.

God is faithful to bring other caregivers into our sphere. What I have found in caregiving is that caregivers tend to accept and affirm each other. We know what it's like; we've been there or are there now. Even the presence of other caregivers is an extension of God's grace and acceptance.

Today you can praise God for this affirmation from Scripture about your core identity. God accepts you. God loves you. And you can accept that as fact!

Dear God of love and acceptance, thank you for gracefully gracing me. When I feel alone, thank you for being present, reminding me who I am in you, and assuring me of your grace. In Jesus's name, amen.

Reflection: Sometimes we look for affirmation from people who cannot affirm us. But God accepts us, and so do others. Who are the people who affirm you, especially now, in this caregiving season? Make a list. Thank God for them. Reach out periodically and connect with them.

26

I AM THE BELOVED OF GOD

Beloved, now we are children of
God. —1 John 3:2 NKJV

The gospel of Luke shares an endearing scene: Jesus is baptized by John. The heavens opened, the Holy Spirit descended upon Jesus, and "a voice came from heaven which said, 'You are My beloved Son; in You I am well pleased'" (Luke 3:22 NKJV).

Spiritual director and author Henri Nouwen describes this moment as "the decisive moment in Jesus's public life . . . when he heard the divine affirmation, 'You are my Beloved.'"[1]

Nouwen further proclaims to each of us, "There is in each of us an inner voice of love that says: "You are the Beloved of God."[2]

When we get caught up in our caregiving responsibilities, it is tempting to begin to anchor our identity to our roles— what we do as caregivers. Let's face it, so much of what we do now orbits around our loved one that it is easy to reduce our entire existence to, "I am a caregiver." Yet, at our core, we are so much more than what we do.

For others, our identity gets summarized by what others say about us. I must admit I took pride in caring for my mother, and it warmed my heart when friends and family members gave me accolades for the care I gave Mom. But we are so much more than what others say we are.

When we receive Jesus as our Lord and Savior, we are transported to the realm of being *in* Christ by the love of God. Loved by God, we become the beloved of God just as Jesus was. Paul addressed Christians in Rome as the "beloved of God, called to be saints" (Romans 1:7 NKJV). That title wasn't reserved just for Roman Christians, but for all who follow Christ.

John, often called the beloved disciple, affirms believers in his epistles by not only calling them beloved, a reminder of their core identity, but then reinforcing it with "we are children of God" (1 John 3:2 NKJV).

You are more than what you do. You are more than what others say about you. No matter how positive those accolades are, they pale when compared to the truth of your core identity. You are the beloved of God: born of God, loved by God, and "accepted in the Beloved" (Ephesians 1:6 NKJV). In you, God takes great pleasure.

Dear God, I embrace your love and thank you for choosing me to be your beloved. In Jesus's name, amen.

Reflection: Consider what it meant for Jesus to be identified as the Beloved of God at the beginning of His ministry. What does it mean for you to be identified as the beloved of God now?

27

I AM GOD'S HANDIWORK

We are God's handiwork, created in Christ
Jesus to do good works, which God prepared
in advance for us to do. —Ephesians 2:10

When I was a teenager, my mom and I learned to crochet. We spent time in our living room crocheting squares. After I went to college, Mom continued making the most comfortable colorful throws from those squares. She sent them to my brother and me for our dorm rooms and gifted them to other family members.

Though we could not pick up this hobby again when she came to live with me, I think fondly about the meticulous care she put into her handiwork. It reminds me that God has put meticulous care and love into each of us, God's children.

After assuring us of God's grace operating in our lives as God's special creations, the writer of the book of Ephesians goes on to describe our unique identity.

We are "God's handiwork." The New King James Version of Scripture says we are "God's workmanship," and the New Living Testament says we are "God's masterpiece."

A particularly poignant message for me is that the Greek word from which each English word is translated signifies a product or a fabric, either literally or figuratively. It speaks of a "thing that is made."[3]

We are God's handiwork—God's beautiful afghan blanket knit together by love for a purpose. Right before this passage, we are told that by grace we have been saved through faith, not by works. Being God's handiwork means God did the work to make us who we are, and not the other way around. We are valuable designer originals, crafted from love with excellence.

As God's handiwork, each of us is made on purpose *for* a purpose. We have been created in Christ to do good works. These works we do are not the essence of our identity. Instead, good works flow from who we are, and are part of God's plan for our purpose.

Have you considered that as God's handiwork, you've been created and crafted for this caregiving task? Caregiving is part of the good works that God prepared for you. When it feels like it's too much, know that God designed you with the capacity to complete this assignment. God crafted you to care and designed you to be diligent. Just as my mother's colorful throws served a purpose for us, you serve a purpose in your own colorful, unique way. And as God's handiwork, you declare and bring glory to God by being you.

Dear God of grace, thank you for making me your handiwork, your unique creation. May all I do bring glory to you. In Jesus's name, amen.

Reflection: Think of how you've been specially created for this task. Celebrate those God-given qualities.

28

I AM VALUABLE

And the very hairs on your head are
all numbered. So don't be afraid; you
are more valuable to God than a whole
flock of sparrows. —Luke 12:7 NLT

Mom gave me her rings for safekeeping when she came
to live with us. She was a minimalist and didn't wear
necklaces and bracelets. But she valued her wedding rings,
a beautiful set with a central diamond solitaire flanked on
each side by two smaller diamonds affixed to a band with five
matching diamonds. I don't know how much this lovely set
was worth. Still, Mom valued it enormously because it represented her marriage to my father and the children born of this
union whom she loved so dearly. For Mom, her rings were
priceless.

We too are priceless to God. As humans, we are created
in the image of God—we are God's image bearers. We hold
the divine nature. In the beginning, God looked out over His
creation, including humans, and saw that it was "very good"
(Genesis 1:31 NLT). God assessed humanity's worth based
on their *being*, not their *doing* or potential. God valued humanity on the basis that He had created them in His image.
Like a valuable one-of-a-kind painting, the human soul is the
canvas upon which God fashioned the divine likeness. As a
human created in God's image, you have inherent worth. You
are valuable because of who you are in all your distinctiveness
and uniqueness.

Caregivers often see the value in others but can fail to see their own worth, that they are worthy of care and support. Jesus tried to get His first followers to embrace this idea of intrinsic worth. He used an analogy of the price of five sparrows, which was a mere two copper coins. The term sparrow can mean any bird "considered good, cheap food and . . . [was] sought after by the poor."[4]

Jesus used a figure of speech centering on a seemingly insignificant bird to show God's providence and care for something others found insignificant. Jesus's point is clear: if God does not neglect even the tiniest bird, how could He forget or ignore you, one who is created in His image?

Jesus says we are more valuable to God than many sparrows. And by using *many*, Jesus doesn't even try to quantify our value compared to these birds, lest His followers make an inevitably incorrect numeric assessment. Jesus is saying to His followers: you are incomparable. God values, sees, and remembers you. Consequently, you can be confident that God cares for you. You can rest assured that God is attending to every dimension of your life, even as you care for another.

God, you value me more than many birds. Help me to appreciate that I am worth caring for because you care for me. In Jesus's name, amen.

Reflection: How does reading that Jesus values you as one of His followers affect your estimation of yourself?

29

I AM RESILIENT

For though the righteous fall seven times,
they rise again. —Proverbs 24:16

It's common for seniors or loved ones with health challenges to become less stable on their feet and fall. As caregivers, we can lessen the fall risk of the one we care for by being mindful of furniture placement, removing rugs, and getting electrical cords and other items out of the walking path.

As I found with my mother, falls still do happen. However, what I really learned from my mother was not the lessons about her falling but her resilience when she got back up! She became the face of resilience, to remind me of my own identity.

Dr. Maya Angelou captured the strength of resilience in her 2009 interview with *Psychology Today*. In response to a question about how we come to know ourselves, Angelou responded:

> Well, I think that we see how we can fall and rise. You see, we may encounter many defeats, but we must not be defeated. It may even be necessary to encounter the defeat, so that we can know who we are. So that we can see, oh, that happened, and I rose. I did get knocked down flat in front of the whole world, and I rose. I didn't run away—I rose right where I'd been knocked down. And then that's how you get to know yourself. You say, hmm, I can get up![5]

Remember, you hail from a faith and culture of resilience. The belief that "I belong on my feet and not my back" emanates from the One who rose from a borrowed grave and forever lives to make intercession for us (Hebrews 7:25). The conviction that "I can get up" stems from a culture of people who did not let enslavement or Jim and Jane Crow keep them down.

Being hopeful and envisioning the power of rising is at the heart of resilience. Dr. Angelou puts it this way: As a people, Black people have remained "intact enough to survive, and to do better than that—to thrive. And to do better than that—to thrive with some passion, some compassion, some humor and some style."[6]

Caregiver resilience is about surviving and thriving with passion, compassion, humor, and style. You have it deep within you to rise from setbacks. You can remind yourself daily, "I am resilient. If I fall, I will get back up."

Dear God of righteousness, thank you for reminding me of the strength you've placed within me. In Jesus's name, amen.

Reflection: Take a moment to reflect on a time or two when you bounced back from a setback. What lesson did you learn? What insight into the strength of your identity can you now glean from that lesson?

30

I AM ENOUGH

So you also are complete through your union
with Christ, who is the head over every ruler
and authority. —Colossians 2:10 NLT

I often felt inadequate as a caregiver, regarding Mom's health
challenges, especially at the beginning of our journey. She
had several chronic conditions that progressed as she aged. It
seemed that each day we faced a new complication.

It wasn't until after she passed that I realized it wasn't her
challenges that made me feel inadequate but my tendency to
want to do things perfectly. Feelings of inadequacy often reveal thoughts of insufficiency or incompetence. There is no
perfect caregiver and no perfect caregiving situation. And
how perfectly (or not) we carry out our role does not determine our worth.

Perfectionism will cause us to strive for an ideal that is an
illusion. Striving for perfection keeps us running on a mental
treadmill, trying to keep up with an image composed of false
expectations. Perfectionism sometimes shows up as our inner
critic demanding that we do more, get more, and sadly, be more.

The truth of the matter, though, is that for Christians, God
has already declared us to be enough. In the early church, this
same myth of perfectionism emerged. Some false teachers con-
tended that Jesus was not fully God and fully human. Consequently, as their teaching went, Jesus was incapable of meeting
the Colossians' needs. Yet, believers could "achieve spiritual fullness through special knowledge and rigorous self-discipline."[7]

Striving for special knowledge and exacting self-discipline kept a person seeking more. God's message to the Colossians is the same for us: in Christ "lives all the fullness of God in a human body" (Colossians 2:9 NLT). Further, because we are in union with Christ, we are complete (v. 10). We are enough.

That message is liberating: we don't need to strive for an illusion to be acceptable to God, and, therefore, to anyone else, including ourselves. Each of us is complete in Christ. We don't have to add anything or do anything to be a person of worth to God.

And as caregivers, we must maintain the mindset that who I am is not contingent on giving care perfectly. I am enough. I don't need to do another thing to be counted as adequate. I am enough because Christ in me is more than enough.

Dear God of fullness, I praise you for filling me and making me complete in Christ. I am indeed enough. In Jesus's name, amen.

Reflection: Spend some time thinking about what you see as your inadequacies. How much of your thoughts are about your value or worth? How might you shift your thinking to align with today's Scripture passage?

SECTION 4

RELATIONAL WELL-BEING

31

LOOK IN THE MIRROR

Now we see things imperfectly, like
puzzling reflections in a mirror, but
then we will see everything with perfect
clarity. All that I know now is partial and
incomplete, but then I will know everything
completely, just as God now knows me
completely. —1 Corinthians 13:12 NLT

I taught Interpersonal Communication courses to under-
graduates at a local university not too long ago. On the
first day of class, I'd ask them to think of someone they'd want
to enhance their relationship with. I instructed them that the
person they'd choose would be the person they'd work with to
complete the class assignments and journaling.

I could almost see the wheels turning in their young heads
as they thought: *Oh, yes! I get to fix this person.* Then I'd let them
know that the first step in enhancing a relationship, any relationship, is growing in self-awareness. The assignments aimed
to help my students grow in knowing themselves. I wonder if,
as caregivers, we too think our relational well-being will improve if only we could fix others around us, including the loved
one for whom we are providing care.

Self-awareness is about knowing and understanding our
own inner state—our needs, desires, strengths, and weaknesses.
It's seeing ourselves, and is fundamental to seeing and relating
to others with empathy and compassion. Yet as psychologist
Dr. Elizabeth Aram is quoted on thriveworks.com, "One of

the most harmful factors in our relationship with others (and ourselves) is our inner critical voice that judges events through past wounds. By understanding these raw spots and practicing self-compassion, we can better relate to others and advocate for what we need in relationships."[1]

For those of us caring for parents or other relatives, current interactions may bring up past wounds, and we find ourselves responding now as if we were still in the past. Being self-aware helps us distinguish between then and now and may even prod us to seek healing of those past wounds through prayer or counseling. We can seek and be open to receiving feedback from others. We also can come to see ourselves as the Holy Spirit reveals our thoughts and motives in light of the Word of God. These are all ways to hold up mirrors and see ourselves more honestly.

We must be intentional about continuing to grow in self-awareness. We can be encouraged to know that though our self-knowledge remains incomplete, God knows us thoroughly and sees us through the eyes of love. God can and will lovingly help us see ourselves and teach us how to relate to others wisely and compassionately.

Dear God of love and compassion, help me see myself through your Word, prayer, and in my relationship with others. In Jesus's name, amen.

Reflection: Take some quiet time to reflect on how you see yourself and how self-aware you are.

32

ONE ANOTHERING

For you have been called to live in freedom,
my brothers and sisters. But don't use
your freedom to satisfy your sinful nature.
Instead, use your freedom to serve one
another in love. —Galatians 5:13 NLT

Years ago, Rev. Richard C. Meyer wrote a series of books for ministries entitled *One Anothering: Biblical Building Blocks for Small Groups.*[2] He turned the phrase *one another* into an active process that encapsulated the relational heart of what God calls us to do with and for fellow believers.

The one-anothering principles apply to caregiving also, especially as relational guides for caregivers. One anothering at its core is about a mutual process of how we relate to one another. Yet they are so much more: they are anchors for our well-being.

According to Jeffrey Kranz of OverviewBible.com, *one another* is used one hundred times in ninety-four New Testament verses. Almost half of these verses give instructions to the followers of Jesus.[3] The essence and power and beauty of the Christian faith, when lived out the way Jesus intended, are found in these one-another principles. These principles or commands speak of building up the community and relationships in the body of Christ.

When the Bible commands us to serve one another, it is given in the context of the believer's call to live in the freedom that comes through the gospel of Christ. No longer bound by a legalistic set of rules, through the grace of God, Christians are free to live their lives following the liberating Spirit.

Being free in Christ gives us the power to choose. The Spirit empowers us to choose actions aligned with God's will for our lives. And it is God's will that we serve one another in love. Caregiving is not about following a set of rules and regulations, although sometimes, with all the schedules, timed tasks, and strict protocols, it may feel like it. Caregiving is about freely loving another, even as we love ourselves.

For caregivers, one anothering may feel lopsided because those we care for most likely are not able to reciprocate in the same way what we share with them. But they do show their love, care, and service as they can—perhaps through a smile, a twinkle in the eye, or a tear that drops in gratitude. The Bible calls for us to love one another (John 13:14, 34, 35), carry each other's burdens (Galatians 6:2), be kind and compassionate to one another (Ephesians 4:32), and be hospitable to one another (1 Peter 4:9).

One anothering is about doing our part, trusting that God will send someone in like manner in our own time of need.

*Dear God of love, you created us to be in relationship,
supporting, caring for, and loving one another. Thank you
for reminding me of my part. In Jesus's name, amen.*

Reflection: Take some time to reflect on what it means to see your caregiving as serving.

33

THE POWER OF AGREEMENT

I also tell you this: If two of you agree here on earth concerning anything you ask, my Father in heaven will do it for you. —Matthew 18:19 NLT

The last thing you need as a caregiver is contention. Though there are plenty of challenges in caregiving, when all parties involved agree, it helps make things easier.

On her very first day on the job, Mom's professional caregiving assistant, Denise, gave me a principle that put all involved in Mom's care in accord: "The focus of care is on what Mom needs." Plain and simple, that was the point of agreement for every nurse, podiatrist, physical therapist, or doctor involved in Mom's at-home care.

It was a unifying prayer for my husband and me. It was the prayer Mom, Denise, and I focused on as we coordinated professional services and trips to hospitals and doctors' offices: "Do what's best for Mom." For us, that meant keeping her mobile with assistance from her walker, and creating a place of love where she felt safe and welcomed.

This notion of agreement stems from the Greek word *sumphoneo*, meaning "harmonious." It can also mean being of one accord. I think of my time caring for Mom and how nurses, physical therapists, and podiatrists all worked in harmony with me and my family to keep Mom active and able to walk. Looking at the Greek word closely, you can see we get our English word symphony from it.

And in many ways, a symphony of care is exactly what we create in caregiving: a symphony of helpers who help you care for your loved one. Every helper plays a distinct role that takes more of the load of caregiving off of you. When everyone is clear on the goal, you create a harmonious process that generates a little more peace for you.

My husband and I agreed with Mom for her daily schedule. She liked to get up early, eat breakfast, and receive her morning caregiver by nine a.m. We adjusted our schedules to accommodate that routine. Often, Denise and I were in agreement as issues arose with Mom's care. Denise and I collaborated, wanting what was best for Mom.

What was so helpful for me was the power that comes with our being of one accord. It made for a harmonious caregiving experience that I look back on fondly.

Today, develop what you need for everyone in your caregiving experience to become of one accord. There is power in agreement.

Dear God of harmony and unity, I thank you for the power of agreement. Show me how to harmonize all of the roles necessary to care for my loved ones, lessening our burden. In Jesus's name, amen.

Reflection: What principle can unite all helpers involved in your caregiving experience?

34

THE GIFT OF PRESENCE

Love each other. Just as I have loved you, you
should love each other. —John 13:34 NLT

One of Mom's favorite shows to watch was *The Waltons*.
Monday through Thursday on her favorite network, she
would watch another story of the intergenerational family
from Virginia who lived on Walton's Mountain during the
Depression era.

Mom's caregiving assistant left each day at noon. I'd get
Mom lunch around one p.m., then head back down to my
home office while she watched her afternoon shows.

One day I decided to start taking my lunch at three p.m.
so that I could join Mom to watch *The Waltons*. Her shows
were so important to her, and I wanted to be with her to share
in something she cared about. I felt that one of the most tangible ways I could show love to my mom was to be present
with her.

I believe that is how Jesus showed love—He was present
with humanity in His incarnation. He was present with sick
people, distressed people, and His disciples. His was the gift
of presence to His first-century followers.

Likewise, the gift of presence today is about our contribution to someone in need. It may be sitting silently with someone in grief. We may listen without judgment to someone
who talks about traumatic events. It can also mean showing
up with a card and a smile at a celebration.

Rarely do we look at our presence with someone else as

a gift to ourselves and a means of enhancing our own well-being while we bless someone else. But we should.

I remember one day joining Mom to watch her beloved Waltons. On that particular day, I fell asleep on the couch and missed a great deal of the show. When I awakened, I looked at Mom in her recliner, and she was in a deep, restful sleep. When she woke, I thanked her for allowing the TV to watch both of us while we slept. We laughed.

There were other times that I watched shows with her, and it enabled me to enter her world and talk about storylines vital to her. It warmed my heart to spend that time with her, listening. I adjusted my schedule to be present with Mom, but the real gift was her presence with me. Her smile, reminiscing and giving the backdrop of stories I wasn't familiar with, blessed my heart.

So, the next time you can adjust your schedule, give yourself the gift of presence with a loved one. You might nap together or you may sit quietly with your loved one and listen. But being present in the moment will bless your heart and cement a lasting memory that will be a gift that keeps giving.

Dear God, help me to be present in the presence of my loved one. Being present slows me down and connects us in ways that enhance our well-being. In Jesus's name, amen.

Reflection: What might you do to give the gift of presence this day?

35

FAITHFUL PRAYING FRIENDS

Then they came to Him, bringing a paralytic
who was carried by four men. And when they
could not come near Him because of the crowd,
they uncovered the roof where He was. So when
they had broken through, they let down the bed
on which the paralytic was lying. When Jesus
saw their faith, He said to the paralytic, "Son,
your sins are forgiven you." —Mark 2:3–5 NKJV

There are times in caregiving when we just seem to hit a wall. Because of the packed nature of the caregiving life, you may feel unable to get to Jesus.

In providing care for others, I have experienced that reality. In some cases, I gave and gave and failed to attend to my needs, and found myself stuck. My tendency then was to blame myself for not being a good caregiver. Or for making a poor judgment call that affected me and the one I cared for.

In those times, I am thankful for faithful friends who could push through the crowded noise in my head with words of comfort and truth. I am grateful for my friends who carried me in prayer to Jesus. These friends helped me uncover the lies I had bought into about myself and the situation. Instead, through their words of wisdom, clear-headed support, and faithful prayers on my behalf, they helped me experience a breakthrough that allowed me to lay a burden at Jesus's feet.

Caregiving can never be a solitary task. In addition to the possible home-care aids and medical professionals that help you support your loved one, you need a group of praying friends who will support *you*.

You may think you don't have time to assemble such a group or to stay in touch to keep them abreast of your prayer requests, but you can't afford not to. The Lord did not mean for us to live the Christian life in isolation. The demands of caregiving can leave you vulnerable and in need of your own support.

Identify your praying sisters and brothers and let them know your prayer concerns. Let them know how they can support and lift you up in their prayers. When you don't have time to call each person individually, you may create an email or text list of four praying friends and send a 911 prayer alert: "I need prayer."

When we are honest about our needs, I believe, just like in the story of the paralytic man, Jesus will see and honor your friends' faith.

Dear God, thank you for never being so overcrowded with other people's needs that you won't hear the requests of my praying friends on my behalf, or my own pleas. In Jesus's name, amen.

Reflection: Who are trusted praying friends you can ask to pray for you? If you already have your prayer group or prayer partners, what is a current request they can be in prayer about with you?

36

GIVING CARE PRECEDES CAREGIVING

This makes for harmony among the
members, so that all the members care for
each other. —1 Corinthians 12:25 NLT

Caregiving is the term used to describe the formal relationship of being a caregiver to a loved one, whether family,
friend or perhaps even a stranger.[4] Our official role is to support an aging or ill person who needs to sustain their life.

I started a caregiver blog while caring for my mom and asked
guest bloggers to share their experiences. Many of those guest
bloggers and I became formal caregivers for mothers, fathers,
or spouses when they aged or became ill. Formal caregiving
often entailed bringing our loved ones into our home, creating
a loving space, and securing medical and other professionals for
their well-being. Sometimes being a caregiver meant being the
primary advocate for a loved one in a nursing home or hospital.

Yet, my husband reminded me that I "gave care" to my
mother long before she moved in with us. All three of us,
her children, did. My dad died twenty-six years ago, making Mom a widow at the relatively young age of sixty-five.
My mother was fiercely independent. She and her younger
sister, Aunt Lucy, also a recent widow, moved in together.
They lived their best lives with their other two sisters in
western Pennsylvania. They all hung out together, shopped,
went out to eat, and of course, they loved attending church

together. They became the core of the Golden Girls at our family's church.

As my mom and Aunt Lucy aged, my sister, Jocelyn, began to help around the house, doing light housekeeping and shopping. Josh, as we call my sister, and her husband were the parents of four young children, and they helped Mom and Auntie. Mom and Auntie also helped my sister and her family. That's giving care.

After Aunt Lucy passed, Mom continued to age but desired to live by herself. My sister, her husband and children, and some cousins remained the local support for Mom. My siblings and I each played roles in Mom's support system. I became the point person for her medical issues. My sister would call and ask me to work directly with the doctors or during hospitalizations. My brother Joe stepped in and handled her finances and holiday excursions to his home with his wife and daughter. That's giving care. That's love.

Giving care and demonstrating love for our family members start well before the formal caregiving role. Those memories can help sustain us in the challenging times that occur now. And for those not fortunate enough to have had the most loving moments with a family member we are currently caring for, we ask God for the grace to call upon past expressions of love from others. Rest assured that those bonds of love prepared us to be a vehicle of God's love for someone else now.

God, who cares for and keeps us, thank you for instilling the impetus of care long before our formal caregiving began. In Jesus's name, amen.

Reflection: Reflect on earlier caring moments and celebrate the bond of love established well before this formal caregiving season.

37

THE (W)HOLY KISS

Greet one another with a holy
kiss. —Romans 16:16

Almost every day, I'd kiss my mother. Sometimes as she
was seated in her lift chair, I'd bend down real close to
her and give her a prolonged kiss on one of her cheeks. She'd
smile. When I tucked her in at night or helped her out of bed
in the morning, I sealed each action with a kiss.

For first-century Christians, the "holy kiss" was significant.
The term is found in four places in the New Testament (Romans 16:16; 1 Corinthians 16:20; 2 Corinthians 13:12; and
1 Thessalonians 5:26), each closing an epistle written by the
apostle Paul. He used the term to encourage unity and love
among the believers in the fellowships.

The kiss is called 'holy' to distinguish it from a sexual
one.[5] New Christians were often "ostracized from family and
friends" in the New Testament church. For these believers
welcomed into the new family of God, "a holy kiss would
communicate a familial closeness."[6]

In 1 Thessalonians 5:23 we are given insight into the state
of being holy: "Now may the God of peace make you holy
in every way, and may your whole spirit and soul and body
be kept blameless until our Lord Jesus Christ comes again"
(NLT). Here wholeness and holiness are interrelated.

Following this passage, as caregivers, "we can connect holiness with wholeness, in that holiness is not a set of dos and
don'ts for us to follow but a journey of becoming whole and

healthy in our spirit, soul, and body as we draw closer to God. I also believe holiness and wholeness entail receiving and experiencing the peace of God."[7]

My kisses to my mother were "wholly kisses"—they were healing for her and for me. My kisses told her she was welcomed, and our home had become hers. My kiss conveyed to her that, in her later years, she was now a loved part of my family and she had a safe place to be whole in her spirit, soul, and body.

Those kisses were wholly for me too. Our time together was sacred, and Mom's reaction to my kiss warmed my heart and spoke to the whole woman I was becoming in this season. As caregivers, we help create conditions for wholeness, well-being, and healing for our loved ones and us. To be free enough to express our love in tangible ways takes caregiving from being a mere transaction to becoming transformational—a radical change from the inside out.

Today, take a moment, if you haven't already done so, and give your loved one a big, wholly kiss.

Dear God of transformation and wholeness, I thank you for your sacred space and for the gift of love that changes us from the inside out. In Jesus's name, amen.

Reflection: Besides wholly kisses, what other communications and expressions might you share with your loved one that speak of wholeness for you and between you?

38

THE RIGHT PERSPECTIVE

"Honor your father and mother."
This is the first commandment with
a promise. —Ephesians 6:2 NLT

Becoming a caregiver for an elderly parent can be challenging. I often mused: being a caregiver for a strong Black woman is no joke.

Though I was here to care for her, I, her eldest child, could never (and would never) forget that she was still the mother. In my family and the families of people from my cultural background, we heard that said many times growing up—if we dared get sassy or smart-mouthed. In other words, they were telling us, "Don't ever get so grown that you lose respect for me as your mother!" Or, to put it more bluntly, "Don't think I can't still put you in your place."

My mom needed a lot of care but had a strong will and sharp mind. Sometimes we'd clash—after all, I'm a strong Black woman who is the daughter of a strong Black woman. As caregivers to aging parents, loving them now entails respecting them for the people they've been and the people they've now become. It means appreciating that God gave those of us who care for aging parents a unique ministry of care, compassion, and respect for those who gave birth to us or adopted us and raised us.

My mom still liked to direct her life. At first it frustrated me because she'd remind me of things to do for her that I knew good and well to do. For instance, "Jeanne, make sure you put my sweater out for me." Or "Watch that I don't roll over the cord of my oxygen tank with my walker." Well, of course I was going to get her sweater out, and no, I wouldn't let her run over her oxygen cord. I didn't think she needed to remind me of these and many other things she would tell me to do.

And then it dawned on me. Mom's mind was still quite sharp, with just a little forgetfulness. And she still was asserting agency, as much as she could, given her required level of care and assistance. That was a good thing. She was maintaining her choice and personal power. I began to celebrate that!

There's a balancing act as the caregiver tries not to try to become the parent, no matter how much care the parent needs. To the extent possible, we can help them to assert agency. We can ask questions about what they want. We can give them choices for meals. We can provide them with options for TV watching. We can ask them what they'd like to wear, even though we will be helping them to dress.

For many years they directed their own lives, as well as ours and other family members' lives. Now, we can help them hold on to that for as long as they can.

Dear God, thank you for our parents. Thank you for the privilege of caring for and serving them in this very challenging time in their lives. In Jesus's name, amen.

Reflection: Write out specific ways to honor your parent or loved one, even as you care for them.

39

BOUNDARIES (PART 1)

The lines have fallen to me in pleasant places;
yes, I have a good inheritance. —Psalm 16:6 NKJV

Boundary management was a practice I had to learn while caregiving. I am still learning. Consider it on-the-job training. I could not care for myself and my mother and still let boundaries remain fluid and crossable by others.

In Psalm 16, the psalmist describes the blessings of God and likens the scope of those blessings to a property boundary line. Just as property lines serve as boundaries for land, "We need to set mental, physical, emotional, and spiritual boundaries for our lives."[8] Boundaries are the invisible lines or rules we set to help define and distinguish us from others.

Maintaining boundaries as a caregiver can be tricky, as we want to care for our loved ones so badly. When their sight diminishes, we help them see. When their dexterity erodes, we begin to cut their food and sometimes even feed them. If we are not careful, we will try to attend to the needs of our loved ones twenty-four hours a day, seven days a week. That expectation and the unwritten rules are not only unsustainable but are a recipe for disaster—ours and theirs.

First, we must identify the things we can do as a caregiver. We never want to do for others what they can do for themselves. Though limited in their capacity, we must identify and respect what our loved ones can do for themselves. Doing so helps to sustain their dignity and autonomy, though it may be limited. It also helps preserve our energy.

Next, we need to identify what is our responsibility and what is not. For instance, many of our loved ones have extensive medical conditions. Trying to become a medical care-provider is sometimes tempting because we are with our loved ones daily and see what they experience. Suppose we notice something going on with our loved one. In that case, we must resist trying to diagnose it and seek a consult from a medical professional. Sometimes we feel that we call out to the professionals too frequently, but clarifying the boundaries between our responsibilities and theirs will be better for you and your loved one in the long run.

In the next devotion, we'll explore clarifying boundaries with other people we are in relationships with. Effective boundary management can make our work as caregivers more pleasant.

God of mercy and love, help me to clarify and manage the boundaries necessary for me to care well. In Jesus's name, amen.

Reflection: Think about the two caregivers' boundaries discussed in this reading: control and responsibility. Which one has been more problematic for you? Spend some time reflecting on that, and develop a set of "rules" to follow.

40

BOUNDARIES (PART 2)

The lines have fallen to me in pleasant places;
yes, I have a good inheritance. —Psalm 16:6 NKJV

So many of us have extensive relationships outside of our caregiving role. For me, caring for Mom became a priority and I had to shift and set additional boundaries in my professional and personal life. I still loved others, but I recognized that I only had a limited amount of time, energy, and emotional reserve for those relationships.

Here are some boundaries I put in place while caring for my mom.

I set client calls to not start until after 9:30 a.m. I needed the morning to prepare Mom and to collaborate on the day with her care assistant when she arrived. Sometimes I had to make exceptions and schedule a call or training session earlier. In that way, I didn't make my boundaries too rigid, yet I honored that morning start time as much as possible. The regularity helped me plan and helped me avoid feeling overloaded at the start of the day.

I had to reduce the number of hats I wore. In addition to caregiving and being a wife, I served as a mentor. I assisted in pastoring our church along with my husband. I had to suspend mentoring for a season. As much as I delighted in pouring into younger women, that role stretched me. I also would have preferred to catch up more regularly with my girlfriends, but I had to put boundaries around those friendships as well. They all understood, having been caregivers themselves in some form or another. Thankfully, our friendships weren't dependent upon weekly check-ins or calls. And when we could chat, we picked up right where we had left off.

I had to accept that some people who weren't as close to me might be upset, or that their feelings could be hurt when I said no or not now to a call or request for a meeting. I believed they would get over it and come to accept the boundary. I had to release myself from angst over saying no or not now.

I learned that those who could not accept my boundaries and chose to separate themselves from me had drawn their own boundary line. They decided they could only be in a relationship with me on their terms and not in a way I could consent to. I determined to pray for them and keep moving.

We accept people where they are and as they are and recognize that our mutual choices set healthy boundaries for us all.

Dear God of love, give me the wisdom to accept the boundaries needed in this season. In Jesus's name, amen.

Reflection: Do an inventory of your relationships. Which ones are guided by healthy boundaries and which are not? What might you need to do to make these relationships healthier?

SECTION 5

MENTAL AND INTELLECTUAL WELL-BEING

41

ON MINDFULNESS

Be still, and know that I am
God. —Psalm 46:10 NKJV

Mental well-being encompasses developing the mindset and thinking patterns critical to caring well. What we think shapes what we do.

During the beginning of the COVID-19 pandemic, when most of us were under stay-at-home orders, I heard a segment on National Public Radio by Dr. Su Varma that helped shape my thinking about my mental wellness. Dr. Varma spoke about strategies for singles or people who live alone to manage loneliness during the stay-at-home orders. I found that what she said was also relevant and valuable to caregivers. She identified four components of mental well-being, the first of which is mindfulness.

Mindfulness is the ability to pay attention and focus. The American Psychological Association reviewed studies on mindfulness and shared the benefits of "mindfulness that is developed through mindfulness meditation—those self-regulation practices that focus on training attention and awareness to bring mental processes under greater voluntary control and thereby foster general mental well-being and development and/or specific capacities such as calmness, clarity and concentration."[1] When left unchecked, so many thoughts can run loose in our heads and cause us to get anxious, worried, or nervous. This mental wandering can drain our energy or make us feel like we are in a tizzy.

As caregivers, we need to take time throughout the day and settle ourselves, get still, and pay attention to what is happening around us and inside us. Prayer, meditation, and breathing exercises are means of being mindful.

For the believer, being mindful is also about connecting to God and what is happening in our spirit. It is about being present in the presence of God. In today's Scripture we are admonished to "Be still, and know that I am God." When we find our minds all over the place, or when we go to pray and can't seem to focus, we need to settle ourselves. We must attend to the now and stay present in the moment. We can pay attention to our breathing and pray for the breath of the Spirit of God to breathe through us. It helps!

Too often, as caregivers we think we are too busy to attend to our mental well-being with even a simple practice that enhances mindfulness. We can't afford not to attend to our mental well-being. We can do it with self-compassion and acceptance.

Dear God, who is ever present with me, help me become present to you in each moment. In Jesus's name, amen.

Reflection: Deep breathing, prayer, and mindfulness meditation are a few practices to help us to become more present in each moment. Which of these might you adopt to help you be still and know that God is present?

42

CAREGIVING IS LIKE . . .

Jesus also used this illustration: "The Kingdom
of Heaven is like the yeast a woman used in
making bread. Even though she put only a little
yeast in three measures of flour, it permeated
every part of the dough." —Matthew 13:33 NLT

In Matthew 13, Jesus uses six similes to describe the kingdom
of heaven. Each of these similes gives a picture of what the
kingdom is heaven is like.

On one particularly trying day, a simile became revelatory
for me. On that day, I woke up late and rushed through devotions. I thought I had prepped Mom's breakfast the day before but had not, so I cooked breakfast from scratch. After his
workout, my husband ran a quick errand to pick up clothes
from the cleaners. He returned home before the caregiver but
later than I had planned. I had forgotten it was the day to refill Mom's pill packs for the week. That took more time. And
of all days, the caregiver was late. My window for my workout
had closed.

Frustrated, I sullenly reflected that "caregiving is like a conductor trying to direct trains that are all running off schedule."
Yes, that was a simile. And it shows the power of language to
help us understand our mindset. I approached caregiving as
a conductor in control of trains and not as a person working
with other humans. I was spending my time and energy trying to control things that were inevitably out of my control.
On the one hand, my propensity for planning is good and

helpful, but taken to the extreme, this "gift" can lead to my trying to control other people (which is impossible), and to extreme frustration.

I couldn't control when Mom would have another ailment. I couldn't control the times when my husband combined errands with his workout and was delayed in returning home. And I couldn't control it when the caregiver was running late. Those things happen. However, I *can* control my perspective and shift my language to describe my caregiving.

I now try to liken caregiving to a slinky toy. Remember those walking spring toys from childhood? Then they were made of lightweight metal; now, they are made of plastic and come in assorted bright neon colors. We'd place one end of the slinky on a step and then tilt the other end over the step and let it go. It would flex and "walk" down the steps, slowly flipping end over end.

Flexibility is key for me and you as caregivers. A slinky is flexible, as we need to be. Blessed are flexible caregivers, for they shall not get bent out of shape. And in their caregiving, they shall reflect the kingdom of heaven.

*Dear Lord, help me to flow with the Spirit and
learn to flow with the other people and situations
in my life. In Jesus's name, amen.*

Reflection: For me, caregiving is like . . . (Create your own simile.)

 Scan this code to view a personal message about this devotion from the author, Jeanne Porter King.

43

ADMIT IT

Through whom also we have access by faith
into this grace in which we stand, and rejoice in
hope of the glory of God. —Romans 5:2 NKJV

When I first started posting about caring for Mom on social media, I was delighted and surprised at the responses.

One group of people who responded to my messages of hope were current caregivers. People from this group often responded with, "I really needed this today." As a fellow caregiver, I understood the difficulties that came with caregiving.

The responses that surprised me came from people who had been caregivers. Their responses often were of this nature: "You'll get through this. I did, and so will you." I was often taken aback by those remarks. I felt judged for voicing my experiences, as if there was a secret code to caregiving, especially for mothers, that I had violated. The unspoken rule was that a caregiver accepted the burden and did not complain.

The funny thing is, I didn't see myself as complaining. My posting was an outlet for sharing and processing my own experience. And writing of one's experience will often touch others and provide a means for them to identify and recognize that they are not alone in their experience.

The third group of people who responded to my posts, usually in private, through a phone call or email, really helped me. They'd admit, "Taking care of my mother was hard." And each one would add something to this effect: "Let me know if you ever want to talk. I'm here for you." Or they'd say, "I am willing to come and sit with your mom to give you a break." Those words felt like confessions of personal truths whispered in secret. It's as if these friends could only admit what it was to care for their loved one to a fellow caregiver who could understand the weight of caring . . . and not judge them as bad caregivers for expressing their own truth.

Everyone's experience of caregiving is different. And it could be that those who responded blithely to my posts did not have a difficult time. But those who acknowledged the difficulty did not deny their love for their parent, child, or friend. Their admission revealed they were humans grappling with the complex dynamic that is caregiving.

It's OK to admit that caregiving is challenging or tedious. That doesn't mean you won't continue to provide the best care you can for your loved one. But that admission can release you from the false notion that something is wrong with you for thinking it's challenging. Admitting that caregiving is complicated is the first step in recognizing you need help yourself. With that admission, you will gain access to the grace from others you need for shouldering the weight of caregiving.

Dear Lord, thank you for the grace to admit that caring for my loved one can be complex and challenging at times. In Jesus's name, amen.

Reflection: Take some time tonight to list people who may be able to assist you in caring for your loved one. Pray about finding a support group or retreat for caregivers.

 Scan this code to view a personal message about this devotion from the author, Jeanne Porter King.

44

DON'T GIVE UP

We have troubles all around us, but we are not
defeated. We often don't know what to do, but
we don't give up. —2 Corinthians 4:8 ERV

Caregiving can be extremely stressful and anxiety provoking. Sorting and administering meds, listening for breathing patterns, and coordinating the care team. Maintaining and sticking to a schedule that has little room for flexibility while yet needing to remain flexible because of the constant changes in a loved one's daily health status. All of these can build up like pressure in a pressure cooker.

In the above passage, the apostle Paul referred to the trials of ministering the gospel, especially in adverse conditions and circumstances. The core of this message is that God gave us a new way of living, and we are to reject deceptive, shameful practices (1 Corinthians 4:1–2). In this way of ministering, God shines a light into our hearts. That light is a source of power from which we live and serve.

This message is not just for pastors and preachers, those we typically think of as ministers. As caregivers, we minister to our loved ones in the most practical ways. Those repetitive acts of service we perform for our loved ones day in and day out, on a schedule that we can't control, can cause us to feel pressured and out of control.

When people feel too much pressure and get overwhelmed, they can shut down, give up, or short-circuit. Yet this passage says that even when we experience overwhelming pressure, we don't have to be crushed by it. Even when we don't know what to do, we can't give up. Quitting is not an option. So what should we do? We may not give up or quit, but we may need to stop and regroup and draw from the power source that enlightens our hearts.

While caring for my mom, I found that I felt the most pressured when I didn't stay present in the moment and allowed the anticipation of seemingly never-ending tasks to stress me. Yes, the ones we care for need us. And we need to recognize that the only way we will make it through the pressures of caregiving is to release that pressure to the One who can ultimately handle it. Often the tension builds as we expect to be perfect in caregiving. It's not perfection we need but power. We caregivers must tap into the power of God, knowing that the "excellence of the power" to provide care is of God and not something we do in our own strength (4:7 NKJV).

When the pressure builds, quitting is not an option, but stopping is. When you feel that pressure build up, stop. Stop and examine your expectations of care. Stop and examine the pressure triggers. Release the pressure valve through prayer, working out, or journaling. You, indeed, do have a treasure within. You are a fragile earthen vessel (4:7 NKJV), but you are not a quitter.

Dear Lord, when I feel pressured, help me stop to talk to you about my pressure triggers. Help me let go of my expectations of perfection and instead embrace being present. In Jesus's name, amen.

Reflection: I won't quit today, but I will stop and get present, then release the pressure by _____ (fill in the blank with the activity you will use to release pressure).

45

RENOVATE YOUR THINKING

Throw off your old sinful nature and your
former way of life, which is corrupted by lust
and deception. Instead, let the Spirit renew
your thoughts and attitudes. Put on your
new nature, created to be like God—truly
righteous and holy. —Ephesians 4:22–24 NLT

I used to be plagued with thoughts of the past. Things I didn't
get right. Mistakes I made. People I may have offended, but
I wasn't really sure. Today, if I'm not careful, I am more plagued
with thoughts of the future. Will I have enough retirement savings in my accounts? Who will care for me when I get older?
What will this world be like in twenty years?

The constant whirling of thoughts can cause you to get
stuck. It takes your attention away from the present and, I
believe, from the presence of God. There is absolutely nothing you can do to change the past. And you can't control the
future. But what *is* in your power is to focus on right now. You
can repent now of your past mistakes and sins and then let
them go, trusting that God, who is so gracious, forgives your
sins. You can pray about your future and ask God for wisdom
for today's decisions that will impact your future.

But you must trust God, who holds the future. The above
passage reminds us to let the Spirit renew our thoughts and attitudes. Thoughts and attitudes are connected. Your thoughts

affect your mood and perspective toward those around you and yourself. Often, a bad attitude comes from an accumulation of negative thoughts about one's past, others, and oneself.

Spiritual renewal of our thoughts and attitudes is like renovating a home. We can remodel a room—paint the walls, paint the cabinets, buy new furniture, and change the light fixtures. It looks good, but really, it's a surface change. But renovation entails gutting the structure—removing the old cabinets, removing the walls, and creating an entirely new design.

That is what today's passage says the Spirit does when He renews our thoughts and attitudes. The Spirit doesn't just tack a few Scriptures on top of our already faulty thinking and bad habits. The Spirit comes to renovate our minds. The Spirit identifies and removes the old thought patterns that keep us stuck in the past or fixated on the future. The Spirit removes the old structures of thoughts that tend to cause us to make faulty assumptions about others and ourselves.

Today, ask the Holy Spirit to reveal those broken thought cabinets that hold your negative attitude. Ask the Holy Spirit to show you the old attitudes that need to be discarded, and the new thinking you need to adopt that aligns with God's mind, heart, and will for your life. This type of deep renovation is a lifelong journey but is taken one step at a time.

Dear Lord, I have allowed faulty thinking and old patterns to clutter my mind for too long. I've hoarded unforgiveness and accumulated anger over a past that I cannot change. Today I ask you to show me the places needing your healing touch. In Jesus's name, amen.

Reflection: List ways to forget the past so you can renew your mind and thoughts.

46

RESPECT YOUR LIMITS

We, however, will not boast beyond measure,
but within the limits of the sphere which
God appointed us—a sphere which especially
includes you. —2 Corinthians 10:13 NKJV

Each of us has been given a sphere of ministry or service in which we operate. Think of your caregiving assignment as a circle where you touch the people within its circumference. The apostle Paul spoke of God's ministry sphere for him and his team. He was determined to stay within those limits and avoid entering other leaders' ministries.

Likewise, we must recognize and accept that God has appointed our spheres of service in caregiving, and some limits come with this. They're for our own good. Those limits are "the naturally occurring circumstances in our lives that constrain what we can do, how much we can do, and how frequently we can do these things before they hinder our mental, emotional, or physical health."[2]

Here are some of the limits I learned to respect while caregiving:

Aging. In caring for my aging mom, I realized I was also aging. I couldn't keep the same pace that I had even a decade earlier. I learned to slow down for my own sake as well as hers.

Time. There are only twenty-four hours in a day. No matter how pressing all the tasks seem, we can't stuff thirty hours of work into our days. When we continually stretch the limits, we get stressed out and become overloaded, overworked, and overwhelmed. We can't care well in that state.

Space. I realized I could only be in one place at one time. And I needed to be fully present. For instance, I blocked out my work calendar for the day when I had to take Mom to her doctors' appointments. Trying to be available to clients while sitting with Mom at her doctors' appointments was too stressful for me.

Death. We only have so much time in this world with our loved ones. Creating those memories with my mom in the moment became so important to me. I committed to living mindfully with her. I sensed that when God called Mom home, I could stand on the fact that I did everything I could while she was here. Those memories and that commitment to love would remain long after she departed.

Respecting limits in my life is for my well-being.

Dear God, I am thankful for the naturally occurring limits you've placed in my life for my well-being. I ask you for the wisdom and grace to respect those limits. In Jesus's name, amen.

Reflection: What's one limit you respected today? What was the outcome of respecting that limit?

 Scan this code to view a personal message about this devotion from the author, Jeanne Porter King.

47

COMMEND YOURSELF

But in all things we commend ourselves as
ministers of God. —2 Corinthians 6:4 NKJV

As caregivers, we get so busy attending to those in our
charge that we don't take enough time to positively note
what we've accomplished and are currently doing. The apostle
Paul called this positively taking note of our accomplishments,
commending ourselves. By commending ourselves, he wasn't
talking about bragging or boasting about ourselves. He was
talking about taking note of what we've been able to accom-
plish as caregivers by the grace of God.

We don't often think about the value of commending ourselves. In fact, some people read Paul's words in this passage as
him bragging about all he had accomplished in ministry. But
let's look at this more closely.

He states that he and his ministry partners commend
themselves as ministers or servants of God. Then he lists almost thirty conditions they faced in serving that proved their
authenticity as servants. They demonstrated patience, met
needs, experienced tribulations "by the Holy Spirit, by sincere
love, by the word of truth, [and] by the power of God" (vv. 4–7
NKJV). They endured evil and good reports; survived deceivers,
chastening, and extreme economic conditions; and remained
faithful.

Paul says we don't need a letter of commendation because
our perseverance through these extreme ministry conditions
is our commendation. Paul and his leaders were committed

to the care of those entrusted to their ministry. The ministry and the people they served were all the commendations they needed.

That's how it is for us caregivers. For every sleepless night, every visit to the doctor's office or emergency room, every prepared and served meal, the commendation or evidence of your service and commitment to care is your loved one. To commend yourself is to note what God has accomplished through you. It's to take note of how far you've come.

It also is thanking God for sustaining you and getting you through your caregiving assignments. You've had to learn new tasks. You've adjusted your schedule, and some assignments have turned your life around. You've rearranged your house, life, and perhaps even your career. This commendation is about thanking God for the grace to change and the strength to persevere. Commending yourself also means taking note of how you've grown. The essence of the Greek word that the apostle Paul uses in this passage means *to stand together*. You, your loved one, and your family are to be commended for standing together through every caregiving trial and test.

Take time today to journal all the ways the Lord has blessed you to care, persevere, and make life better for the one entrusted to you. Write those things out as a memorial to God's faithfulness and your growth and commitment.

O God of love, thank you for reminding me of how much I've been able to do by your grace. I take time now to celebrate and thank you for this caregiving journey. In Jesus's name, amen.

Reflection: As you reflect on this day, write about where you see growth in your caregiving.

48

MAKE THE INVISIBLE VISIBLE

Share each other's burdens, and in this way
obey the law of Christ. —Galatians 6:2 NLT

There's a concept in gender studies in which married women tend to take on more household duties in their homes than their husbands, even when the woman works and has a career outside the home. Even when spouses do take on more work at home, the woman typically organizes and takes the responsibility for managing the household. That additional unpaid work is called invisible labor.

I found the same thing to be true in caregiving—regardless of marital status. For many of us, our loved ones cannot manage their affairs, let alone the day-to-day activities of their lives. We take on this management task in addition to running our households and working. While everyone can see the physical labor we expend in assisting with grooming, doing laundry, and helping our loved ones get in and out of bed, few people recognize our mental work.

For instance, we ensure that tasks for their care get done. We organize care assistants and see that they get paid on time. We schedule doctors' appointments and deal with the logistics of getting our loved ones to these appointments. We do this while managing our work and households and remaining compassionate and loving to all we encounter. It can be mentally draining.

Invisible labor is sometimes called mental load, and caregivers pay a toll for carrying it while caring. Caring under the weight of that invisible labor hampers our well-being, if not managed well.

The Lord admonishes us, in today's Scripture passage, to share each other's burdens. Clearly, as a caregiver, you do that. But who shares the invisible labor of caregiving with you?

One of the things we must learn to do as caregivers is to talk about the hidden labor we perform and enlist people around us to help with this burden, thereby relieving us of some of the mental load.

As you manage care of your loved one, remind other members of the family (spouse, children, extended family) that it's time to share management of the household. Often we do what we do so well and hide that invisible labor, so that others remain quite comfortable letting us carry it all.

Now is the time to make the invisible visible, asking others to share this load. You will be glad you did.

Dear God, help me identify family and friends who can help. Please enable me to make this invisible load visible by sharing it with you. Give me the words to share with others. In Jesus's name, amen.

Reflection: Make a list of people in your life who can begin to organize and manage critical assignments that will relieve you of some invisible labor.

49

BEND, DON'T BREAK

They are like trees planted along the
riverbank, bearing fruit each season. Their
leaves never wither, and they prosper
in all they do. —Psalm 1:3 NLT

I love the old song "I Shall Not Be Moved." The writer
described being like a tree planted by the waters and not
being moved. To not be moved, in this sense, is to be like a
tree that withstands the storms of life and is not uprooted and
does not break.

This song speaks of the steadfast conviction of the caregiver that regardless of what comes our way, we shall not be
moved. We shall not be uprooted. We shall not break.

In an article about the steadfastness of trees in New Hamp-
shire, writers for the Forest Society describe how these trees
survive extreme weather conditions in the northeast: "As the
snow piles up, you may see trees bent over with their crowns
nearly touching the ground, leafless and haggard."[3] These trees
can't escape the extreme weather conditions, yet they survive.

Likewise, as caregivers, we can't escape the extreme caregiving conditions. Yet, the imagery of Psalm 1 suggests that
we can *thrive* and not just survive.

But how?

We can learn from the survival strategies of these trees: they
have adapted over time to deal with heavy rain, wet snow, or
ice that threatens to weigh them down and even break them

down. Spruce trees, for instance, "simply bend or fold branches to shrug off snow."[4]

Isn't that marvelous imagery for us caregivers? There are times when we must bend to the will and needs of our loved ones. Sometimes, we must shrug off ill-timed comments from people who don't know about our situation. There will even be times when we must shrug off the cold reality that we want to quit. But we can't, and we won't.

We must learn to flex in our thinking and mentally adapt to the changing conditions of caregiving. We must accept that some stormy, uncertain seasons will threaten our resolve and commitment and even break us down.

In those seasons, as the psalmist describes, we must see ourselves as people who delight in the Lord, meditate on God's Word, and draw strength within to keep going. For it is that time with God, the time in the Word, that can help keep our minds open, our wills pliable to the will of God and flexible in our circumstances. Rigidity cannot be central to caregiving.

Today, make up your mind. By God's grace and with the Lord's help, you are like that tree that has learned to adapt to its circumstances, flourishes in due season, and refuses to be moved by the vicissitudes of the caregiving life.

Dear God, plant me right here, in the center of your will. Please give me the resolve not to be moved from my assignment. In Jesus's name, amen.

Reflection: Take some time to identify areas in your caregiving where you may need to bend (or adapt) more to ease the strain on you.

50

FIX YOUR THOUGHTS

And now, dear brothers and sisters, one final
thing. Fix your thoughts on what is true, and
honorable, and right, and pure, and lovely, and
admirable. Think about things that are excellent
and worthy of praise. —Philippians 4:8 NLT

For a while, I woke up every morning wondering if Mom
was still alive. I worried that she would pass in her bed
at night. I often felt anxious about her chronic illnesses and
concerned that she would die on my watch. Or that I would
do something that would complicate her condition.

Yet on the other hand, I asked God not to let her suffer
through a long, drawn-out illness. I couldn't bear the thought
of my mother suffering through excruciating pain.

Then as some of her illnesses progressed, with every new
issue that arose, I wondered if I would be able to continue to
care for her at home. I thought there would come a time when
I would need to secure more help, or place her in a care facility
because of her condition.

Worrying and overthinking can be so draining and peace-
sapping. One day I heard the Spirit whisper in my heart, "Your
mom came to live with you, not die on you." That message
shifted my thinking from worrying about her death to being
present in her life. Our thinking can shape how we feel, what we
choose, and, ultimately, what we do. No wonder the apostle Paul,
in the book of Philippians, admonishes Christians to fix their
thoughts on positive things—things that are true, honorable,

right, pure, lovely, admirable, excellent, and praiseworthy. These positive thoughts enhance inner peace.

Today, psychologists reinforce the message found in this Bible passage. The Mayo Clinic staff report, "Having a positive outlook enables you to cope better with stressful situations, which reduces the harmful health effects of stress on your body."[5] Some benefits of positive thinking include increased life span, lower rates of depression, better psychological and physical well-being, and reduced risk of death from certain illnesses.[6]

So how do we "fix our thoughts" on positive things? First, we catch or become aware of the thoughts that do come into our minds. We must note our tendencies toward positive or negative thinking. We must shift our perspective if our thoughts tend toward the negative. We must ask ourselves, "What is another way to think about the situation?" Then we must be intentional about practicing that new, more positive thought.

As caregivers, we cannot control what goes on around us, but we can, with God's help, control what goes on inside of us.

Dear God of peace, help me to bring my thoughts into alignment with your Word and to recognize the true and beautiful things in my situation. In Jesus's name, amen.

Reflection: Take a quick inventory of your thinking about your loved one. Are your thoughts more positive or negative? What might you do to fix your thoughts on positive things?

SECTION 6

EMOTIONAL WELL–BEING

51

BE RESPONSE-ABLE

A person without self-control is like a city with
broken-down walls. —Proverbs 25:28 NLT

Emotional well-being is about expressing emotions in healthy ways in our relationships and roles. It is easy to be emotionally reactive and driven by our feelings. It takes more discipline and self-control to attend to our emotions—listen to what they may be telling us about what's going on inside of us—and to use those cues to develop healthy responses without overreacting.

When I first discovered the above Scripture passage, the image of the broken-down walls really grabbed me. If we are overly reactive and not maintaining self-control, we risk opening ourselves and others to harm; we are much like an unprotected city. So, we must work on slowing down and being more intentional about responding.

In his classic book, *The 7 Habits of Highly Effective People*, Stephen Covey provides insight into the difference between responding and reacting. He parsed the word *responsibility* into its two parts and emphasized that "response-ability" is "the ability to choose your response."[1]

As caregivers, we have a choice about how we will respond to what is happening around us.

Responding is a choice, whereas reacting is something we do immediately without any conscious thought of choice, as if on automatic pilot. Depending on the gravity of your loved one's condition, caregiving can be stressful, and stress makes us more prone to fall back into reactionary mode. We've got to be able to recognize when we go there.

According to Covey, reactive people are "driven by feelings, by circumstances, by conditions, by their environment."[2] Response-able people are "driven by values—carefully thought about, selected and internalized values."[3]

It doesn't always work this way, but for the most part, response-able caregivers choose our responses to situations, focus on what we have control over, and collaborate with people to help us make the response-able choices. Reactive caregivers, on the other hand, focus on the deficits of others, even of those we provide care for. Reactive caregivers blame, shame, and complain, creating negative energy to which others will react.

The good news is that the Holy Spirit can and will produce the fruit of self-control within us (Galatians 5:22). Self-control can blossom in our lives when we are mindful of what is happening inside us at the moment. To do that, we must practice slowing down. We must pray, asking the Spirit for guidance in our situations, and seek proactive strategies and contingencies. When the unexpected arises and it stresses us, leaving us feeling out of control, we can imagine that the walls of our lives are guarded by God. Though we feel out of control, God is still in control—not our feelings.

Dear God of protection, keep my heart set on you—even when it is filled with many emotions; help me guard against overreacting. In Jesus's name, amen.

Reflection: Take a moment to reflect on what responding and reacting look and sound like for you. What may be a cue to attend to when you slip into reaction mode?

52

GOD CARES ABOUT YOU

Give all your worries and cares to God, for
he cares about you. —1 Peter 5:7 NLT

With the incessant demands of caregiving, we sometimes forget a vital truth of our spiritual life. God cares for us. Or let me be more direct: God cares about *you*.

Yes, you. God cares about the whole of you. God cares about your soul, the innermost part of your being. God cares about the physical you. God cares about the mental and emotional load you carry.

And God is present to offset your load.

In today's Scripture reading, the apostle Peter writes to Christians suffering because of their faith commitment. His words of assurance are relevant for all of us who follow Christ.

Peter reminds us to "give all your worries and cares to God." The Greek word we translate as *cares* denotes "distractions, anxieties, burdens, and worries," and in practical terms, it means "to be anxious beforehand about daily life."[4]

This passage reminds us that while we are caregivers of our loved ones, God is our caregiver. Just as we tend to the daily needs of the ones entrusted to us, God tends to our daily needs, especially the spiritual needs that strengthen us for the journey.

And just as you spend time with the loved one you care for in your daily transactions and activities, you must spend time with your "Caregiver," allowing the Lord to strengthen you from the inside out.

When we insist on carrying the cares and burdens of the

caregiving life by ourselves, we are prone to stress, burnout, and distractions. Instead, each day we must give these cares to God before they become burdens that weigh us down.

This day, carve out time to pray, and give your cares to God. When care issues arise that threaten your peace, talk to God about it. God will help you.

Recognize things you've become anxious about that are out of your control. Give those things to the One who is in control.

Dear God, I cannot carry these cares alone; I need you to take them. I need your help caring for my loved one, and I trust you to guide me in this caregiving assignment. In Jesus's name, amen.

Reflection: Today, how can you give one of your cares to God?

53

COMBATTING COMPASSION FATIGUE

Why are you cast down, O my soul? And why are
you disquieted within me? —Psalm 42:5 NKJV

Caregivers are susceptible to compassion fatigue—"the physical, emotional, and psychological impact of helping others—often through experiences of stress or trauma."[5] It can come upon us suddenly or build up over time. When we are unaware of the dynamics inside our soul, we are less likely to recognize the feelings of emptiness that have set in until they manifest in very stark ways. When it occurs, we can feel, like this psalmist, very cast down, discouraged, and disquieted.

The psalmist does something, however, that we all must regularly do to become or remain aware of what's going on inside us—interrogate our soul or heart. We must listen and attend to what is bubbling up inside of us so that we can become aware of our internal undercurrents.

Symptoms of compassion fatigue can be physical—such as broken sleep, lethargy, and diminished energy. They can also include sadness, emptiness, agitation, and extreme loneliness. Symptoms may even include behaviors such as avoiding connecting with others. If you experience any of these, take some time for self-care, including contacting a therapist for assistance.

Once very early in my caregiving journey, I snapped while talking to my brother-in-law. I had never done that before, and we both knew then that I was feeling overwhelmed. I didn't have a name for it at the time, but I suspect I was experiencing some compassion fatigue. Caregiving was new. Attending to my aging mother's needs was a privilege, but it also pushed me to my limit.

I had to take stock of what I was experiencing, and of my triggers. My trigger at that time was trying to be a *perfect* caregiver for my mom. I tried to attend to Mom's every need and be present for every request. I thought I was serving from a place of compassion. But my compassion tank was nearing empty, and I was failing to take time to refill it through acts of self-compassion (see Devotion #56).

Thankfully, Mom saw what was happening too, and she outlined for me what she could and wanted to do to help *me* help her. I began to set more realistic expectations for myself. For instance, I pulled together a morning schedule that worked for her and me—giving me time for prayer, reading, quiet time, or working out before I got her up.

I settled into caregiving without draining my levels of compassion and care for Mom.

Perhaps you too recognize feelings of being overwhelmed and other emotional responses to being overloaded. Becoming aware of your feelings and the beliefs that drive you to push to the brink of exhaustion, and then adjusting, will go a long way toward helping you combat compassion fatigue.

God of my heart, help me recognize what's going on inside of me, leading to fatigue. Be my strength and re-energize me. In Jesus's name, amen.

Reflection: What is your soul saying today?

54

GOD'S COMPASSIONS NEVER FAIL

Because of the LORD's great love we are not
consumed, for his compassions never fail.
They are new every morning; great is your
faithfulness. —Lamentations 3:22–23

We may experience compassion fatigue, but God won't. The prophet Jeremiah looked around and heavily identified with the suffering of his people. Their suffering drove him to lament over what they endured. No wonder he is called the weeping prophet. Yet, at some point, Jeremiah stopped looking at his distress and looked to God. Only then could Jeremiah acknowledge that though his compassions were being drained, God's compassions would never run out. God's love toward the people was replenished every morning. And God's people could draw from God's store of love and compassion each new day.

Brené Brown, author of *Atlas of the Heart*, puts it this way:

> "There's compelling research that shows that compassion fatigue occurs when caregivers focus on their distress reaction rather than on the experience of the person they are caring for. Focusing on one's emotional reaction results in an inability to respond empathically to the person in need. . . . We're not hearing the story; we're inserting ourselves in the story."[6]

Isn't it amazing that what may drain us the most is empathizing so heavily with another person's suffering that we stop hearing their story and start inserting ourselves into it? And doing so drains our well of compassion, which will run dry if it isn't replenished through the life-giving love of God. Jeremiah knew this from experience. He proclaimed to the people of his land that they had forsaken the spring of living water and had "dug their own cisterns, broken cisterns that cannot hold water" (Jeremiah 2:13).

What a powerful image for us. In our brokenness, we try to care from a place of compassion. Yet we focus on ourselves and may have some critical and condemning thoughts. If we do not draw from the life-giving love of God, we will care from broken jars that can't hold water. In other words, our broken assumptions, motives, and dreams affect how we care. Sometimes we operate out of the brokenness that God wants to heal, even as we care for our loved ones.

We draw from God's compassions when we spend time in God's presence, pray to Him for strength, and just sit still and soak in the grace of God. His compassions are overflowing—there's enough for the person we provide care for and for us. God's compassions never fail to reach us. They never fail to fill us. And they never fail to heal us.

Today, take your eyes off your own caregiving distress and focus on the overflowing compassions of God.

God of compassion, God of love, fill, fuel, heal, and hold. I trade in my broken cistern for your living water. In Jesus's name, amen.

Reflection: What's one thing you did today to exchange a broken cistern for God's life-giving compassion?

55

NO CONDEMNATION

So now there is no condemnation for those who
belong to Christ Jesus. —Romans 8:1 NLT

In the heat of the moment, I said some things that hurt Mom.
I felt terrible after it was brought to my attention, and I apologized and asked for forgiveness.

Yet I ruminated upon the situation for some time afterward. *How could I be so thoughtless? I was careless with my words.*
I condemned myself with accusatory thoughts and judgment.

Please know that none of us will be perfect caregivers; we all make mistakes. We may even hurt the feelings of those we love. The enemy's lies will heighten negative interactions and turn them into condemning thoughts and accusations.

One of the fundamental tenets of the Christian faith is that we are saved from the penalty of death, hell, and the grave because of what Christ did for us on the cross at Calvary. We are justified and counted righteous when we receive Christ as Lord and Savior.

We who belong to Christ Jesus, who are in union with Him, are not condemned or judged as guilty. Yet if we are not careful, we can experience condemnation and guilt over things we do, or fail to do, especially as they relate to caring for our loved ones. We must apologize and ask for forgiveness when we offend or hurt someone. And then leave it there.

We also must learn from our failures and grow. We cannot beat ourselves up and go to a place of self-condemnation.

God has freed us from condemnation, and we must be willing to free ourselves from guilt.

Pay attention to the words you think or say about yourself in a situation where you've fallen short and missed the mark. For instance, thoughts such as "I should have known better" lead to self-blame and disapproval about what you didn't know or do. Blame and disapproval are never good motivators for caring, nor do they help us become better caregivers.

Instead, we have to move from condemnation to commendation (for more on commendation, see Devotion #47). Too often, out of the one hundred things we've done well as caregivers, we let one wrong word relegate us to "bad caregiver."

Instead, we must learn from our mistakes and grow as we learn. To paraphrase Dr. Maya Angelou, you can tell yourself, "Now that I know better, I will do better."[7]

Today I encourage you to let go of self-condemnation and be free to become better.

Dear God of love and freedom, thank you for saving me from my words and thoughts of condemnation. I look to you for truth and freedom. In Jesus's name, amen.

Reflection: Pay attention to your words or thoughts about yourself, especially after a mistake or failure. Write them down, then replace them with learning, growth, and encouraging words.

56

SELF-COMPASSION

Therefore, as God's chosen people, holy
and dearly loved, clothe yourselves with
compassion, kindness, humility, gentleness
and patience. —Colossians 3:12

In the early stages of caregiving, my mother helped me clothe
myself with compassion. Because I juggled many demands
and expectations from my clients and church, Mom saw, with
patience and understanding, how hard I worked to care for her.

She reminded me that I didn't always care for myself during those early days. Just when I thought I was dropping one
of the metaphoric balls I was juggling, she said, "Jeanne, you
are doing such a good job caring for me. I really appreciate
you." Or she'd say, "Now, sweetie, slow down. You keep running up and down those steps to see about me. I'm OK, and
I'll call you when I need you."

Slowly it dawned on me that Mom was coaching me on
showing as much compassion for myself as I was offering her.
She was helping me clothe myself with compassion.

We are admonished to "clothe [ourselves] with compassion,
kindness, humility, gentleness, and patience" as God's chosen
people who are holy and dearly loved by God. The clothing we
are to put on, including self-compassion, flows directly from
God's love for us.

The admonishment to clothe ourselves with compassion
reminds me of the guidelines we hear when flying. The flight
attendant reviews the safety procedures: "In the case of an

emergency, and the oxygen masks are deployed, put your mask on first before trying to assist another with their oxygen mask."

Isn't that the same thing? Before we try to love someone and be compassionate toward others, shouldn't we ensure that we are fully dressed in compassion? Shouldn't we love ourselves in healthy ways? In so doing, don't we demonstrate to others that we can likewise love them in healthy ways?

Self-compassion is part of the emotional side of caregiving, and most of us are not trained on the emotional side of caregiving. Yet the emotional skills of setting and maintaining boundaries allow us to develop healthy habits such as getting adequate sleep, keeping our doctors' appointments, going for a walk, or exercising. Developing these healthy habits is a way of being compassionate toward ourselves—giving ourselves the care, attention, and love we need to be whole.

Let's not love others in the nude. Let's dress with compassion and learn to be gentle with ourselves, showing kindness and making time for self-care.

Dear God of love and grace, thank you for choosing me and giving me the proper clothes of compassion to love myself and others. In Jesus's name, amen.

Reflection: Imagine an act of compassion as if it were an article of clothing. List one piece of clothing you must wear today to be compassionate to yourself.

57

WHEN YOU'VE HAD ENOUGH

> Then he went on alone into the wilderness,
> traveling all day. He sat down under a solitary
> broom tree and prayed that he might die. "I
> have had enough, LORD," he said. "Take my
> life, for I am no better than my ancestors who
> have already died." —1 Kings 19:4 NLT

The caregiving life can be a solitary one. There are lots of challenges and many victories. Every day that we get through health challenges and flare-ups, the bureaucracy of healthcare, and many things that are out of our control, we can count as a victorious day.

Elijah the prophet had just had a dramatic showdown with the prophets of Baal. He was victorious. Yet victories are draining. After the adrenaline drops, there's an empty feeling, and we are more prone to feel threatened and make poor decisions.

Consequently, Elijah ran from a threat and found himself alone in the wilderness, ready to die. He sat down under a tree and declared that he'd had enough. No matter how strong you feel as a caregiver or how many wins you achieve, there will come a time when you will feel as though you've had enough.

It is in those times that we can appreciate the next steps God took Elijah through.

Elijah lay down and slept. Then he ate some fresh bread

and drank some refreshing water. Elijah lay down again. He then ate some more and then restarted his journey.

Sometimes, when we feel we've had enough as caregivers, it's time to take a break and accept that enough is enough. It's time to lie down, sleep, eat, and sleep some more.

Whether on a vacation or staycation, caregivers need time to regroup, become restored, and tend to themselves. We need the space not just to sleep but to sleep in. We need to be able to eat and eat some more. We need to be able to sit under a tree and do nothing.

If you find yourself so empty that you feel suicidal, then get help now. Call the national suicide prevention hotline at 988. God sent Elijah divine help in the form of an angel with food and water. God can help you by providing professionals for you to talk with.

Before you get there, though, ask family members and friends for help. You've had enough and need a break.

Dear God of more than enough, please give to me from your abundance when I've had enough. I pray for your holy touch to guide me. When I've had enough, give me the courage to make the right call. In Jesus's name, amen.

Reflection: Imagine that "enoughness" could be measured on a scale from one to ten, one being low, or "I'm in a good place," and ten being "I'm done. I have had enough." Where are you? If your level of "enoughness" is too high for you, what might you need to do to reduce it?

58

GOD OF THE VALLEYS

The man of God came up and told the king of
Israel, "This is what the Lord says: 'Because
the Arameans think the Lord is a god of the
hills and not a god of the valleys, I will deliver
this vast army into your hands, and you will
know that I am the Lord.'" —1 Kings 20:28

Yesterday we read about a great victory that Elijah experienced atop Mt. Carmel. Forty days later, Elijah arrived at Mt. Sinai, the mountain of God. The prophet Elijah had great mountaintop experiences.

Mountains are beautiful places that highlight God's incredible creation. Spiritually, they represent a victorious place in God or being close to God.

We yearn for mountaintop experiences in our lives. We long to hear from God, to see and realize the evidence of God's presence in our lives. Especially as caregivers, we need to know that God is with us, directing and guiding us.

But life, especially the caregiving life, includes valley experiences. We've come to associate valley experiences with the low moments in our lives. We may enter a valley when we receive bad news from the doctor, or when, despite all our care, our loved one takes a turn for the worse. We sometimes feel low when circumstances are out of our control.

We must remember, though, that the God who is God of the hills and mountains is also the God of the valleys.

In one of its many battles, the people of God in ancient

Israel defeated their enemies atop a mountain. The following year, their enemies decided to attack the Israelite nation in the valley because they falsely believed God was God of the mountain but not of the valley. God assured the people that they would defeat their enemies because God would show up in the valley despite the false belief of their enemies.

We too must be reminded that God is not limited by place or space. In our most significant moments of joy, God is with us and is God. And in our lowest moments of sorrow, even in the death of a loved one, God is still God.

Today, remind yourself that you may have mountaintop highs and valley lows in caregiving. But one thing remains certain: God is with you during your mountaintop experiences and in your valley experiences.

Dear God, thank you for the reminder that wherever I am, you are right here with me. In Jesus's name, amen.

Reflection: Take stock of where you are right now. Praise God right where you are, knowing that He is with you.

59

CATALYZING ANGER

Human anger does not produce the
righteousness God desires. —James 1:20 NLT

You will get angry if you are not careful to keep caregiving
in perspective. You may become angry with your loved
one for needing so much of you, especially if the person you
care for was not present when you needed him or her in the
past. You may experience anger with family members you
had hoped would help but haven't for whatever reason. And
you may even grow angry with God for choosing you for this
assignment. Feel your anger. Own your anger. But don't let
anger own you.

Unmanaged anger can take a toll on our mental and physical health. Express your anger to a counselor, spiritual director, or God. But be careful not to act out of anger with your
loved one. Brené Brown, a bestselling author and professor of
social work, describes anger as "an emotion that we feel when
something gets in the way of a desired outcome or when we
believe there is a violation of the way things should be."[8]

When you come to understand and accept at some level
that your irritation may stem from feeling your own desired
goals have been blocked, you can choose what to do with that
emotion. You can also choose to adjust your goals. For example, you may come to understand and accept that your tendency to get annoyed with your elderly loved one's repetitive
question is because, at some level, you don't believe this is the
life you chose for yourself. You can choose to empathize with

your loved one and realize that they probably didn't choose this life either.

But here you are. Caregiving while holding down a business. Caregiving while raising children by yourself. Caregiving for someone who wasn't the most caring toward you. You may feel that putting your life on hold isn't fair. But you can't let anger engulf you and eat you inside. Anger is so complex. Perhaps underneath your anger is regret for not being closer to the one you now care for. Perhaps you are grieved over losing the vibrant person you once knew. Or maybe your anger is the pain of having to see your loved one suffer.

Brené Brown teaches us that "anger is a catalyst . . . an emotion that we need to transform into something life-giving: courage, love, change, compassion, justice."[9] Unmanaged, unbridled anger does not produce God's righteousness. But understanding your anger can help you transform it into righteous action. How might you channel your anger into righteous action that helps you and your loved one? Pray and ask the Lord to show you.

Dear Lord, help me understand my anger and not use it to hurt the one I care for. I don't want this anger to eat me up. Thank you for hearing my heart, loving me through this, and giving me the outlet to express my frustration. I pray for your grace and love to flow through me. In Jesus's name, amen.

Reflection: Today I felt anger when_____.
Here's what I did with my anger:_____.
Here's what I will do the next time I feel this anger:

_____.

60

THE JOY OF THE LORD IS YOUR STRENGTH

And Nehemiah continued, "Go and celebrate
with a feast of rich foods and sweet drinks, and
share gifts of food with people who have nothing
prepared. This is a sacred day before our Lord.
Don't be dejected and sad, for the joy of the
LORD is your strength!" —Nehemiah 8:10 NLT

Some of the most precious times of caring for my mom were the occasions I would now call sacred moments. These were moments when, for instance, she entrusted a special private prayer request with me or would ask me to delve into a Bible passage with her.

I lead a prayer call for the women of my church every Wednesday morning at seven a.m. Every Tuesday night, as I was tucking her into bed, she'd ask, "Now, tomorrow is Wednesday, right?" I'd respond, "Yes, ma'am." And then she'd say, "It's the prayer call, right?" "Yes, ma'am, it is." She'd then remind me to wake her up so she could join us.

When my mother first came to live with me, I tended to go down to the lower level of our home, where my office was, to take those calls. I didn't want to wake her. I also had all my resources at my fingertips in my office. The first part of my calls is a devotional unpacking of a Scripture passage or short teaching before we pray. But because Mom wanted to be on the calls, I began to lug my Bible, commentaries, notes, and prayer journal to her room. I spread them out on the ottoman or floor so she could participate in these calls.

Still lying in her bed, Mom often would listen to the calls with her eyes closed. To be honest, I sometimes felt she drifted back to sleep during those calls. Feigning indignation, I'd say to her after the call, "Mom, you fell asleep during our prayer call!" She'd perk up and retort, "Oh, no, I didn't. I heard every word. And it was a good call."

Her words brought a smile to my face. I would then turn our morning news show on in preparation for getting her up. Then I'd lug all my resources back downstairs to my office.

The joy in her voice strengthened me each week, knowing she participated in our weekly prayer calls. Those times were sacred between mother and daughter. They brought great delight to both of our hearts and strengthened us for the caregiving journey.

Dear God, your joy strengthens me for this caregiving journey. Thank you for your joy. In Jesus's name, amen.

Reflection: As you look at your daily or weekly caregiving tasks, identify a few sacred moments with your loved one that bring joy to your heart. Write about those moments in your journal. The joy these times bring will strengthen you now and in the future.

SECTION 7

PHYSICAL WELL-BEING

61

YOUR BODY IS A TEMPLE

Don't you realize that your body is the temple of
the Holy Spirit, who lives in you and was given
to you by God? —1 Corinthians 6:19 NLT

Our bodies are sacred containers of the divine. Although we
are more than our bodies and are integrated wholes comprised of spirit, soul, and body, it is in and through our physical
bodies that we live out our lives in this world. In writing to the
church in Corinth, the apostle Paul reminded Christians of the
sacredness of the body. He admonished them against sexual
sins conducted in the body that were antithetical to the Christian lifestyle God calls for.

In denoting the body as a temple, we must also hear the
message not made explicit in this passage but is nonetheless
true. Our bodies are gifts from God, and to not care for them
and attend to our physical well-being is to be poor stewards.
Physical well-being is about the care of the body in terms of
rest and renewal, paying attention to what and how we eat,
and doing physical activities, to name a few things. Just as
pastors, church members, and custodians attend to the upkeep of our church buildings and properties, so must we tend
to the upkeep of our temples.

But how many of us take our physical bodies for granted?
When we shift our thinking to seeing our bodies as sacred
vessels, we will be more inclined to respect the body in all its
complexity. For instance, the human body comprises eleven
interconnected systems that include cardiovascular, digestive,

endocrine, integumentary (skin), lymphatic and immune, muscular, nervous, reproductive, respiratory, skeletal, and urinary.[1] Medical professionals such as internal medicine doctors specialize in our overall care, and specialists tend to the care of specific systems. Just as we ensure that our loved ones get to doctors' appointments, we must make and keep our own appointments for annual checkups or for particular concerns that appear.

There are several things we can do to enhance our physical well-being. The National Institutes of Health has created a physical wellness tool kit[2] to help us develop positive physical health habits. They recommend getting active, maintaining muscle, finding a healthy weight, minding our metabolism, eating a healthy diet, and building healthy habits. Healthy habits for the care of our body include drinking plenty of water, moving, getting plenty of rest, and eliminating or avoiding harmful substances.

Finally, we can celebrate what God does through our bodies. As the ancestors of my faith tradition said at each testimony meeting, "I thank God for a reasonable portion of health and strength." We can thank God for our physical health, though it may not be perfect. We're still here.

Dear God, thank you for creating me with such marvelous complexity. Help me to attend to my physical well-being. In Jesus's name, amen.

Reflection: Take a closer look at the healthy habits given above. Which have you incorporated into your lifestyle? Which can you add now?

62

TAKE A BREAK

Jesus said, "Come off by yourselves; let's
take a break and get a little rest." For there
was constant coming and going. They didn't
even have time to eat. —Mark 6:31 MSG

Sometimes caregiving can feel like such a swirl of activity, with many people coming and going: helpers, home-aid assistants, physical therapists, nurses, and home doctors. Sometimes the swirl is brought about by the daily schedule of activities necessary to maintain your loved one's health: meal prep, medicine prep, grooming, and exercising. Then there is the flurry of activity when they face an unexpected health crisis: calling 911, securing medical transport, waiting in the ER, and accompanying them to their room.

Jesus knew the toll He and His disciples paid due to the heavy demands He encountered as He cared for, taught, healed, and prayed for others. So busy were they, sometimes, that they didn't even have time to eat. I remember on occasion not being able to eat because of the nonstop morning routine of getting Mom out of bed, to the bathroom, and then to her chair while preparing her breakfast and feeding her on time.

I love that Jesus told His disciples, amid the swirl of activity, "Let's take a break." And they found a secluded place. You see, you must take a break from this work, so this work does not break you.

According to AgingCare.com, "30% of caregivers die before those they are caring for."[3] The numbers for Alzheimer's caregivers are estimated to be even higher. According to a Stanford University study, "40 percent of Alzheimer's caregivers die before the patient— . . . not from disease, but from the sheer physical, spiritual and emotional toll of caring for a loved one with Alzheimer's."[4]

With no break, caregivers can suffer from caregiver burnout. They can become so stressed that stress deleteriously affects their mental, emotional, spiritual, financial, relational, and physical health. You can't wait to see these signs of stress; you must plan for breaks as part of your caregiving routine now.

Here are a few things that you can do to help you take a break:

- Consider respite care for your loved one.
- Solicit help from family members.
- Coordinate helpers in ways that give you a block of free time.
- Say yes to volunteers.
- Create a secluded place in your home for brief breaks.

Dear God, I want to be able to take breaks. I pray for your guidance in helping me find a secluded place to rest. In Jesus's name, amen.

Reflection: As you reflect on this passage, identify a couple of secluded places where you can rest awhile.

63

THE LORD WATCHES OVER YOU

I lay down and slept, yet I woke up
in safety, for the Lord was watching
over me. —Psalm 3:5 NLT

When my mother first came to live with us, I set up a camera in her room to monitor her at night. Some of you have similar devices for people you care for, such as "baby cams" for your children.

I would awaken three or four times a night to check the camera. Every time she moved, it triggered an alert. Each time, I'd go to her room and check in on her.

I operated in fear in those early days, causing me to lose a lot of sleep. The enemy of our souls attacks our minds with fear and can tempt us to misconceive that we are in control of our loved one's every breath. We are not.

The above psalm was written by David when he was on the run from his rebellious son Absalom. Can you imagine how heartbreaking it must have been to have a once-favored son now an enemy? Imagine how David must have felt as he fled from his own flesh and blood, who was leading an uprising against him. That was enough to cause David to lose sleep every night.

Yet it didn't. David testifies in this song that he lay down and slept and woke up safely. David attributes his ability to lie down, sleep, and wake up safely to the fact that the Lord was watching over him.

You see, caregiving also can cause us to have sleepless nights. The fear of what-ifs becomes an enemy of our well-being. We can sit up night after night worried and wondering, What if they stop breathing? What if I don't hear them? What if they fall out of bed? As caregivers, we must do all we can to ensure our loved ones are safe at night. But once tucked in safely, we, like the psalmist, must believe and trust that God is watching over us and our loved ones.

In other words, God keeps our loved ones and us. God protects our minds from becoming a resting place of fear. He sustains us through the night when our bodies are rebuilding and rejuvenating through sleep.

With Mom, I eventually became so comfortable that I could suspend the motion alert on the camera in her room. Each night I tucked her in and kissed her forehead, and she was nestled comfortably into her bed, guard rails up. I, too, learned to nestle snugly in bed and sleep. As caregivers, we must find a way to get adequate rest for our well-being.

Pray and ask the Lord to give you a plan to ensure your loved one's safety at night and your ability to rest. Trust that the Lord will wake you up when you are needed. Trust God to watch over you both.

Dear God, I thank you for the assurance and testimony that we can sleep and get rest when we've entrusted our loved one and our own sleep to you. Thank you for the reminder. In Jesus's name, amen.

Reflection: What is one thing you will do to ensure you can sleep well tonight?

64

THE POWER OF SLEEP

In peace I will lie down and sleep, for you alone,
O Lord, will keep me safe. —Psalm 4:8 NLT

In the Bible, there are numerous references to physical sleep, which provides physical rest and recuperation. Sleep is the "regularly recurring condition of body and mind in which the nervous system is inactive, the eyes closed, the postural muscles relaxed, and consciousness practically suspended."[5]

God put Adam into a deep sleep to create Eve (Genesis 2:21–22). We find a stressed Elijah asleep under a juniper tree while running away from Queen Jezebel (1 Kings 19:1–7). Jacob received an angelic dream while asleep (Genesis 28:11–12).

On numerous occasions, Jesus is depicted as sleeping on a boat during a storm (Matthew 8:24; Mark 4:38; Luke 8:23). While Jesus prayed in the garden before His betrayal, the disciples are depicted as sleeping and exhausted (Luke 22:45).

As you see from these few passages, sleep is essential to our well-being. Sleep improves creativity, promotes healing from sorrow and grief, and enables dreaming. Natural sleep is depicted as a gift from God (Psalm 127:2) and reflects a trust in God to care for the one who sleeps.

Social science research concurs with the inherent benefits of sleep. The National Institutes of Health states, "During sleep, your body is working to support healthy brain function and maintain your physical health."[6] According to Healthline, sleep can improve concentration and productivity, strengthen your heart, support a healthy immune system, help to regulate blood sugar, and regulate our emotions and improve social interactions.[7]

Being able to sleep, even amid turmoil, is attributed to the keeping power of God (Psalms 3:5; 4:8). In fact, Psalm 4 is "sometimes labeled an evening prayer due to the references" to sleep and rest.[8] According to the *New Spirit-Filled Life Bible*, verse eight "closes . . . like the fading notes of a lullaby."[9] A necessary part of the human condition, sleep is included in the Psalter as a song praising God for the ability to lie down in peace and rest. Sleep is crucial to our health, well-being, and self-care plan as caregivers.

Today, let's commit to receiving God's gift of sleep. We are designed to rebuild, restore, and replenish ourselves through sleep.

Dear God, I thank you for the gift of sleep. I sometimes get too busy to get the rest I need, so today I ask you to help me order my life so that I can get adequate sleep each night. In Jesus's name, amen.

Reflection: What plans do you need to make to ensure you get adequate sleep?

65

LAUGHTER IS GOOD MEDICINE

A cheerful heart is good medicine,
but a broken spirit saps a person's
strength. —Proverbs 17:22 NLT

At one point in my caregiving, Mom's home caregiver, Denise, came six days a week for three hours in the mornings to assist her. I scheduled many client meetings during this time and ran errands if needed. One day, I told Mom, Denise, and my husband that I was heading out to run some errands. Honestly, sometimes just driving around in my car was a great getaway.

When I returned after my trip to the post office, Walgreens, and our local grocery store, I entered the house with a cheerful, "Hey everybody, I'm back!" Denise said, "Hi!" My husband came down to help me unload the car.

Mom called out from our family room, "Jeanne, come here a minute, please."

"Sure, Mom," I responded. "Let me take off these outside shoes first."

I scurried down to where she was to see what she wanted, anticipating that she needed me to do something for her.

I drew closer where she sat comfortably in her chair and asked, "Hey, Mom, what's going on?"

She looked at me real close and said, "I just needed to see you. I haven't seen you in a while." Now mind you, she said this with a totally straight face. But I got it. I laughed and said, "Oh, Mom, are you trying to say I was gone for a long time?"

"Yes, that's exactly what I'm saying!" And then she joined me in laughter.

I'm here to tell you no one can "signify" better than a Black mom. Signifyin' is a Black communication trope of indirection. It is used to make a point without *actually* saying what is meant. And I received the message Mom was sending: I was gone longer than she expected, just running errands. Together, we had a great laugh.

Maintaining a sense of humor and being able to laugh with each other, even at ourselves, is excellent medicine for the soul. It's also good medicine for our overall well-being. According to HelpGuide.org, a site for mental health and wellness, "Laughter strengthens your immune system, boosts mood, diminishes pain, and protects you from the damaging effects of stress. Nothing works faster or more dependably to bring your mind and body back into balance than a good laugh."[10]

Find ways to bring laughter into your caregiving. Find comedy shows you and your loved one may like. Call out funny things that happen during the day. Look for humor, even in adverse situations. Remember the fun. Laughter is a free, readily available medicine that does us all good.

Dear God, thank you for reminding me to laugh. Help me to find humor in even challenging situations. In Jesus's name, amen.

Reflection: Start a humor journal to write down the fun things that happen during your caregiving. Review it from time to time to give yourself a great laugh.

66

WALK IT OUT

That same day two of Jesus' followers were
walking to the village of Emmaus, seven
miles from Jerusalem. As they walked along
they were talking about everything that had
happened. As they talked and discussed these
things, Jesus himself suddenly came and began
walking with them. —Luke 24:13–15 NLT

After one of my mother's hospitalizations, she needed to
transfer to a rehab facility. We chose one about a mile
and a half from our home. On days that I wasn't transporting
laundry to or from her room, or it wasn't too hot outside, I'd
walk to see her.

Walking is one of the most beneficial self-care practices and
is especially helpful for caregivers. According to Ashley Zlatopolsky—a contributor to RealSimple.com, a lifestyle site—consistent, regular walking can improve heart health, lower stress
and improve mood, reduce depression, strengthen joints, control blood sugar, and boost immune function. She sums it up:
"[Walking] can help you maintain healthy weight, metabolism,
blood pressure, and blood cholesterol, all of which help keep
your heart healthy."[11]

In our super mobile society, where many of us rely upon
our cars, buses, or trains to get around, we need to reap the
benefits of walking. In many of the cultures depicted in the
Bible, walking was the norm. People's primary means of getting from place to place was using their feet.

So it is no surprise that in one of the darkest seasons of the disciples' lives, two of Jesus's followers left Jerusalem crestfallen, heading to a village called Emmaus, about seven miles away. While walking and talking about Jesus having been put to death, unbeknownst to them, the resurrected Jesus suddenly shows up and walks with them.

As they walked with Jesus, they could talk it out. It wasn't until after they arrived at their destination and prepared to eat—when Jesus took the bread, blessed, broke, and gave it to them—that they recognized their walking companion.

After He disappeared, they noted how their hearts had burned within while they talked to this "stranger," now made known. After walking it out with Jesus, they could go to the other disciples and declare that the Lord had indeed risen (Luke 24:34).

As caregivers, we need to make walking a habit not just for all the physical benefits but also for the spiritual and emotional benefits. We can be assured that when troubled, if we can walk it out in prayer, Jesus will show up.

Dear God, who walks with us, thank you for showing up for me. Give me the strength and discipline to seek you as I walk through the day. In Jesus's name, amen.

Reflection: How might you integrate walking into your daily routine?

67

GET MOVING

For bodily exercise profits a little, but
godliness is profitable for all things, having
promise of the life that now is and of that
which is to come. —1 Timothy 4:8 NKJV

It is so tempting for us caregivers to forego exercise because
of the demands of our busy schedules. Some of us scurry
around so much that when it comes to our physical well-being,
we are too tired to think about going to the gym or catching a
virtual workout class.

Unfortunately, too many of us came from traditions that
touted spiritual exercise over physical exercise. But as one of
the elders of my tradition once said, "If bodily exercise profits
a little, I want every bit of that little."

In the New Testament, the imagery of athletes exercising
for contests is prominent. Scripture uses runners and athletes
as examples of self-discipline. For instance, the apostle Paul
wrote to the church at Corinth, "I discipline my body like an
athlete, training it to do what it should" (1 Corinthians 9:27
NLT). Likewise, believers were to discipline their entire lives
to earn their spiritual rewards. Thus, the Bible doesn't malign
physical exercise; the writers just remind us to keep it in its
proper perspective.

Today, a time in which we are much more sedentary than
was true of our first-century siblings, physical exercise is a
necessary part of mind-body-spirit well-being. But first we
must demystify exercise.

Exercise is "any movement that makes your muscles work and requires your body to burn calories."[12] Exercise can be beneficial for losing weight, strengthening our muscles and bones, and enhancing cardiovascular health. Regular exercise can help increase energy levels, aid in happiness, and even enhance self-esteem.

We don't necessarily have to invest in a gym membership. Exercise is about movement. Moving through dance, walking, swimming, leg lifts in a chair, stretching, and yoga. We can start small by climbing the stairs instead of taking an elevator or parking the car away from the store and walking farther to the entrance. The important thing for caregivers is to get moving.

Dear God, who created my body, I ask for your help and grace in caring for my temple. Help me incorporate consistent movement into my day so I may care well. In Jesus's name, amen.

Reflection: If you consistently exercise, reflect on the benefits to your mind, body, and soul. If you do not exercise regularly, list one thing you can start today to get moving.

68

BREATHE DEEPLY

The Lord God formed the human from
the topsoil of the fertile land and blew
life's breath into his nostrils. The human
came to life. —Genesis 2:7 CEB

One day, when my husband and I were out running errands, I returned to the car to find him staring at his
watch in the driver's seat. I waited a few moments to see if
he'd respond to me returning to the car. When he didn't, I
quietly asked, "Are you all right?" He looked up briefly and replied, "I'm just breathing." He then showed me the breathing
app on his smartwatch. From that day on, I started practicing
deep breathing.

Breathing is essential to life. Genesis depicts God creating
the first human from the dirt, blowing into earthen nostrils
the breath of life. I imagine God's breath into the first human
was gentle but deep, traveling to the lungs, expanding the abdominal cavity, and traveling back through the mouth. That
breath animated the entire being.

Too often today, we don't pay attention to our breathing
because of our stress-filled, hectic lives. If we did, we'd notice
how shallow our breaths are. We move too fast through our
day to sit still and inhale, deeply filling our lungs and watching the abdomen rise while the lungs expand.

According to the Harvard Health Publishing site, "Deep
abdominal breathing encourages full oxygen exchange—that
is, the beneficial trade of incoming oxygen for outgoing carbon

dioxide. Not surprisingly, it can slow the heartbeat and lower or stabilize blood pressure."[13]

Deep breathing activates the parasympathetic nervous system, which regulates relaxation and reduces the body's stress responses. According to the Cleveland Clinic, "Because of the signals it carries, the rhyming phrases 'rest and digest' or 'feed and breed' are easy ways to remember what your parasympathetic nervous system does."[14]

As caregivers, we are faced with demands that put our nervous system on high alert. We can't sustain healthy lives living under perpetual stress. That is why regularly slowing down and breathing deeply is a crucial self-care practice for caregivers.

There are simple but effective ways to get started even without a smartphone app. You can start by sitting upright in a comfortable chair and expanding your chest. I personally like to lie flat on the floor. Place one hand on your abdomen and one on your chest. Breathe in through your nose, feeling your belly rise; hold it for a few seconds, then release the breath through your mouth. Repeat for one minute. We must make time for deep breathing and use it to offset the effects of our high-stress demands.

God of breath, as you did at creation, breathe through me and relax my body, soul, and spirit. In Jesus's name, amen.

Reflection: Think of the times and places that you can incorporate regular, consistent deep breathing into your care routine.

69

EAT RIGHT

So whether you eat or drink, or whatever
you do, do it all for the glory of God.
—1 Corinthians 10:31 NLT

Each time Mom was hospitalized, before she was discharged, I would meet with the dietitian to see what changes needed to be made to her diet for Mom's nutritional needs. It helped in my caring for Mom, but it was also beneficial for me to be reminded of healthy eating tips. We had different dietary needs but both of us needed to eat right.

Eating right is developing a healthy perspective on food, nutrition, and eating in a way that enhances our overall well-being.

Eating right helps us sustain our physical and mental health. According to the National Health Service (NHS) of Scotland, "A well-balanced diet provides all of the energy you need to keep active throughout the day; [and] nutrients you need for growth and repair, helping you to stay strong and healthy and help to prevent diet-related illness, such as some cancers."[15]

In addition, eating right can help us sustain heart health, maintain strong bones and teeth, and even help us manage our weight.[16] On the other hand, "an inadequate diet can lead to fatigue, impaired decision-making, and can slow down reaction time. In fact, a poor diet can actually aggravate, and may even lead to, stress and depression."[17]

Most caregivers must be meticulous in preparing meals for the loved one they care for, yet too many caregivers ignore our healthy dietary needs. Many of us "stress eat" or eat comfort foods. Most of those foods are high in sugar and salt, which are unsuitable for our bodies.

Eating right includes making healthy choices for meals for our families and ourselves. Eating right also includes mindful eating. *Mindful eating* is defined as "paying attention to how you feel when you eat, and what you eat . . . [and it] is one of the first steps in making sure you're getting well-balanced meals and snacks."[18] Of course, eating right also entails checking in with your doctor and dietary professionals for plans that work best for your health conditions.

As we see in today's Scripture passage, let's do all things to the glory of God—and that includes our choices of food and drink. Let's eat right.

God, who created food for our health and enjoyment,
help me to get the right balance for what eating
right can mean for me. In Jesus's name, amen.

Reflection: Many of us must pay more attention to what and when we eat. Consider keeping a food journal or downloading a food-tracking app to document your eating patterns and gain insight into your eating habits.

70

PACE YOURSELF

Therefore, since we are surrounded by such a
huge crowd of witnesses to the life of faith, let
us strip off every weight that slows us down,
especially the sin that so easily trips us up.
And let us run with endurance the race God
has set before us. We do this by keeping our
eyes on Jesus, the champion who initiates and
perfects our faith. Because of the joy awaiting
him, he endured the cross, disregarding its
shame. Now he is seated in the place of honor
beside God's throne. —Hebrews 12:1–2 NLT

Racing through life was such a habit for me. I didn't even
realize I was running up and down the stairs until Mom's
home-care assistant brought it to my attention. She said, "You're
going to wear yourself out running up and down those stairs like
that." I paused for a moment and caught my breath. I looked at
her and thoughtfully replied, "You're right."

The demands of caregiving can be so great—so much to
do with so little time—that we feel pressured to race through
the day, trying feverishly to get it all done. Thus, many of us
approach caregiving like a hundred-meter dash instead of the
marathon that it truly is. I found that to be healthy for the long
haul of caregiving, I had to learn to pace myself. So will you.

When we approach caregiving (or life in general, for that
matter) as a sprint, our goal is to get through the race quickly
and get it over with. We want to win quickly. We run through
our tasks fast, our minds racing to the following demand and

the next. Our breathing gets shallow, and our hearts race; most of the time, we don't even realize it. We just keep zipping along.

In Scripture, the Christian life is often compared to running a race (see, for example, 1 Corinthians 9:24 and 2 Timothy 4:7). Caregiving is now part of your life of faith. This passage admonishes us to run this race with patient endurance, suggesting our Christian life is a distance race. Running a distance race takes pacing yourself to endure the course. Caregiving requires pacing yourself so that you can travel the path your life is now on.

God knows the race that is set before you—the course that has been designed for you. Sometimes you need to run faster to meet an urgent demand; sometimes, it is best to slow your pace and take your time. Other times, you'll need to stop and take a break. Ask the Lord to set your pace for all you will face today and each day.

Dear God, I look to you for guidance. Help me to pace myself through this day—not running too swiftly or too slowly. Help me to stay in step with you as you order my steps throughout this day. In Jesus's name, amen.

Reflection: Where do you feel it in your body when you start moving in overdrive? Do you feel winded? Do you feel your heart racing? Do you inadvertently hold your breath? Those are physical reminders for you to slow down. What can remind you to pace yourself when you've started rushing through caregiving?

VOCATIONAL WELL-BEING

71

WON'T BREAK MY SOUL

*And what do you benefit if you gain the whole
world but lose your own soul? Is anything worth
more than your soul?* —Matthew 16:26 NLT

Because of the pandemic, in 2022, 70 percent of C-suite executives seriously considered resigning for a job that better supported their well-being.[1] In June of the same year, music icon Beyoncé released the song that became a workplace anthem for many people: "You Won't Break My Soul." Academics, media moguls, and corporate leaders echoed what many of us caregivers already knew: working through challenging life circumstances can exact a toll on our souls. Consequently, many people started reassessing careers and jobs and have explored "vocation" to clarify their purpose and how to live it out.

Vocational well-being is the ability to maintain a sense of fulfillment from the work and activities we feel called to do. It involves being able to steward our resources and gifts well. Many of us as caregivers have known for a while that our roles at work are not our only major responsibilities. To be well and care well, we must listen to our souls and align the many roles we hold with the health of our souls. My friend Connie Lindsey calls it "connecting your soul with your role."[2] I call this getting soul-role alignment.

Too many of us can get so caught up in the whirlwind of working and caregiving that we feel like we are losing our souls—our peace of mind, our equilibrium. The first thing we can do as caregivers is get a vision for our vocation. Vocation is broader than our jobs and speaks to a more profound calling for and about our lives. In the next devotion, we'll look more at this notion of vocation as a calling. As we become clearer on vocation, we can better understand where our current paid work fits in with our commitment to caregiving.

Next, we can set priorities for what is important to us. Based on those priorities, we must choose where to spend our limited time. Few of us have the choice to quit our jobs and not work. In fact, "African-American caregivers are the most likely racial/ethnic group to be in the labor force (sixty-four percent)."[3] But some of us must choose how we might work differently in this season of life.

Then, we must prayerfully develop a strategy for harmonizing our work and caregiving. Doing so might include asking for more flexibility at work to meet caregiving demands.

Though workplace demands have shifted significantly since the pandemic, as caregivers, we must take the lead in cultivating our vocational well-being to enable us to care well for our loved ones and ourselves.

God, who calls and equips us for vocation, help me gain clarity on my roles and their effect on my soul. Help me creatively prioritize work and caregiving. In Jesus's name, amen.

Reflection: Take some time to sit with the notion of soul-role alignment where you bring your work, caregiving, and life into alignment. What does that mean for you? How might it shape your priorities?

72

CALLED TO CARE

Therefore I, a prisoner for serving the Lord, beg
you to lead a life worthy of your calling, for you
have been called by God. —Ephesians 4:1 NLT

Sometimes, as Christians, we limit the idea of calling to vocational ministers, such as pastors or preachers who have
accepted ministry as their full-time profession. Yet Scripture
indicates that God has called us all and wants us to live lives
worthy or exemplary of that calling.

Noted author and spiritual leader Parker Palmer captures
this notion of calling in his book, *Let Your Life Speak: Listening for the Voice of Vocation*. In chronicling his journey to
finding his true calling, he shares insights that are particularly
helpful for us as caregivers.

He shares that we hold values and truths at the heart of
who God made us to be. God uses these core values to guide
us. When we are guided by those values within and not the
voices of other people's expectations, we will hear the voice of
vocation.

Palmer is not speaking of vocation as a job or profession
but as a calling that we hear deep inside. Vocation, "rooted in
the Latin for 'voice,' . . . does not mean a goal that I pursue. It
means a calling that I hear."[4]

Caregiving is a calling. For some of us, God led us directly
into a caregiving profession, or our loved one asked us to care
for them as their health declined. For others, conditions dic-
tated the need for us to step in. Yet whatever the circumstances

that brought us to caregiving, something deep within us spoke to our hearts. It bore witness to our choice to become caregivers.

When we see caregiving as a calling, we realize it is not something we have to do but something we get to do. We have been called to partner with God in providing care and love to relatives, friends, or strangers who cannot care for themselves.

When we see our caregiving as a calling, we accept the distinct life it beckons us into and seek grace from God to live a life worthy of that calling.

Because we are called to care, we have been given a unique opportunity to use our skills, abilities, gifts, and experiences to serve others. To live a life worthy of caregiving is to demonstrate through our actions and attitudes the value of our roles and the people we serve.

Dear God, who calls and beckons, you deemed me able to care and instilled the capacity for caregiving in me. I trust you to care through me. In Jesus's name, amen.

Reflection: Recall how you heard the voice of vocation beckoning you into your current caregiving situation. What does it say to you now?

73

DON'T TRY TO DO EVERYTHING

I can do all things through Christ who
strengthens me. —Philippians 4:13 NKJV

Not long ago, I discussed my heavy workload with a friend. Putting on that strong Black woman persona that many of us know so well, I said, "But I can do all things through Christ who strengthens me!" My friend responded, "But does Christ want you to do *everything*?" I immediately felt that check in my spirit. My friend was right; I misappropriated that Scripture to justify my tendency to do too much.

The Apostle Paul wrote to the Philippians, most likely from a Roman jail, to thank them for their generous contribution. As a missionary leader in his day, the apostle faced many difficult circumstances. According to 2 Corinthians 11:24–28, he was beaten with whips and rods, was stoned, was shipwrecked three times, and he had experienced hunger, thirst, and nakedness. There were times he described his situations as "hard-pressed on every side," leaving him feeling at times "perplexed" and "persecuted" (2 Corinthians 4:8–9 NKJV). In these circumstances, Paul focused on his purpose to proclaim Christ. Because of this focus, he could say he was "not crushed" by circumstances and not "in despair" or "destroyed" (vv. 8–9 NKJV).

When writing to the church at Philippi, Paul rejoiced over the care he received from them. They did what they could to help alleviate the burden of caring for the souls of others. He did not want to speak of his own need. He described knowing how to live in humble circumstances and in prosperity, as he experienced the financial ups and downs of ministry. He experienced hunger and fullness. It is in that context of learning to deal with the fluctuating conditions of ministry that the apostle declared, "I can do all things through Christ who strengthens me."

As caregivers, we minister to the loved ones we care for. And the conditions of our service will vary, sometimes drastically. One moment our loved ones may be laughing, enjoying life with us, and in the next, their minds may trap them in a long-ago past. One moment our loved ones will be walking with the assistance of their walker. Then the next, they fall, requiring emergency medical attention. Those situations are stressful for caregivers, yet we can draw strength from our faith in Christ. We, too, can persevere in caregiving in good times and challenging times.

But what we must not do is misappropriate this Scripture to justify trying to be everything to everybody, and saying yes to every request, ultimately saying no to ourselves.

Dear God of love, mercy, and strength, show me what you want me to do in this season of caregiving. In Jesus's name, amen.

Reflection: Have you used today's Scripture to justify taking on too much? What might you do differently in this season?

 Scan this code to view a personal message about this devotion from the author, Jeanne Porter King.

74

FOCUS ON THIS ONE THING

No, dear brothers and sisters, I have not
achieved it, but I focus on this one thing:
Forgetting the past and looking forward
to what lies ahead, I press on to reach the
end of the race and receive the heavenly
prize for which God, through Christ Jesus,
is calling us. —Philippians 3:13–14 NLT

In the previous devotion, we talked about not trying to do
everything as caregivers. Most of us have added caregiving
into our already full lives. We most likely work, are active in our
churches, have many friends or family members we hang out
with in person or stay connected to by phone or social media.

When the apostle Paul wrote about focusing "on this one
thing," he was speaking of keeping his eyes on the prize of
the upward call of God in Christ Jesus. He likened his call to
a heavenly prize he sought in running this Christian race. In
this way, he illustrates that the Christian life is an active response to God's ongoing call toward himself through Christ.

By focusing on pleasing God in this Christian race, with
our eyes on the prize, what is important becomes more ap-
parent. We come to grips with what we must prioritize in this
season of our lives.

With my heart set on responding to God's new calling on
my life, one of the first things I had to do was to assess where

my family and I were at that time. We were moving Mom in with us during a global pandemic, and my husband had two elderly parents who were needing more attention as they maintained their household nearby. Like all of us, we sought guidance through this pandemic. I ran a now-turned-virtual consulting and training company from my home office.

We had to push past the past and focus on the now. Thankfully, we were able to secure home-care services that assisted me with Mom and gave me time to work. Also, I was working from home, and when the care assistant wasn't on duty, I was not far from Mom. Focusing on the call of God led me to prioritize providing the best care for Mom in the context of working from home. Doing that in a way that pleased God became my priority.

Focusing on caring in a way that pleases God is one thing we must always do.

Dear God, who calls and beckons us to you, you are the prize our heart longs for. Thank you for calling me toward you. In Jesus's name, amen.

Reflection: Assess where you and your family are now. Considering God's call to care in a way that pleases Him, what are your priorities? To whom and how must you convey those priorities?

75

HARMONIZE YOUR LIFE (PART 1)

Live in harmony with one
another. —Romans 12:16

One of the biggest challenges for caregivers is maintaining a balance between their home/personal life and their professional or work life. Achieving and maintaining a work-life balance is an age-old challenge for all professionals, but it is even more challenging for caregivers.

Pastor and life coach Dr. Toni Alvarado admonishes that we should eliminate the notion of work-life balance as it is an unachievable goal. She writes, "I have taught seminars and workshops entitled The Balancing Act, only to struggle with the elusive ideal of balancing my own life."[5]

Dr. Alvarado explains why balancing work and life is not an attainable goal. "The word balance," she explains, "suggests that we are in a constant state of equilibrium with an equal distribution of weight and tension."[6] Picture those measuring scales with a compartment for weighing items on each side. They are balanced when the exact weight is placed on each side.

Work-life balance suggests we can give the same weight to work and home-life demands. As Dr. Alvarado writes, "Life is not easily packaged in equal amounts of experience and responsibilities."[7] As caregivers, there is often so much uncertainty in the demands of our care that, at times, caregiving will require most of our attention and energy. Furthermore, work is part of our lives. The notion of work-life balance privileges work as having an equal part to the rest of our lives.

Instead of striving for the balance goal, Dr. Alvarado coaches us to seek harmony in our lives. Harmony is the "consistent, orderly, or pleasing arrangement of parts."[8] Harmony is the outcome of not having work and life balance but having work and home set in their proper places in our lives, given the onslaught of demands each requires.

To live in harmony, as Romans 12:16 admonishes, is to live in agreement, to live in accord. One translation renders the verse, "Be of the same mind toward one another" (NKJV). To live in harmony is to develop an overarching mindset that reflects values or principles by which we order our lives.

No wonder the apostle encouraged his readers to renew their minds. Harmonizing our lives as caregivers begins with the right mindset. In the next devotion, we will look at three necessary elements to help us arrange our caregiving lives to achieve harmony.

God of harmony, help me keep the various parts of my life in their proper perspective. In Jesus's name, amen.

Reflection: Take some time to rethink the notion of work-life balance for yourself. List the various components of your life. How does work fit into your life? What values guide you in making decisions about work and caregiving?

76

HARMONIZE YOUR LIFE (PART 2)

Live in harmony. —Romans 12:16 NLT

In the previous devotion, we examined the myth of work-life balance. As we saw, the notion of work-life balance suggests that work and the rest of our lives are in equilibrium, with each component of our lives placing equal demands on us and requiring equal amounts of energy, time, and focus. As caregivers, we know that's not true.

Many of us may recognize the concept of harmony from music. Picture the praise team or choir at your church that sings in three-part harmony: the sopranos, the altos, and the tenors. Each section sings its part, following or accenting the main melody. Likewise, achieving harmony in our lives as caregivers will require following and accenting the melody, depending on the demands placed on us at the time.

God sets the melody for our lives in terms of giving us purpose, principles, and values that guide our lives. We chart out those notes or principles in the strategies we develop to prioritize our tasks and activities, including self-care. For instance, a core value that has anchored me for most of my life has been faith and family first. I also attempted to strive for excellence, another value, in all I did. Professional excellence, for instance, is an outgrowth of my faith.

The values we live by remain implicit when things are going well. We go on autopilot, handling the demands of home, work, school, and so on. When demands conflict, however, we experience discord. That is when we must examine the core values or principles that guide us and use them to make decisions to bring our lives into harmony. It will mean making a high priority of some things and putting others on the back burner. And it would help if we learned to be OK with the fact that we can't do it all equally.

During my caregiving season, as work demands increased along with home caregiving, I set Mom's care as a top priority. I rearranged the other needs of my life around her care. As I wrote in Devotion #40, I had to set new boundaries for clients, which meant hiring more contractors to meet client demands.

Your life situation no doubt is different from mine, but you can use this principle to help write the musical score for your life. God reveals His purpose for each season, and as you listen to the melody in your heart, as informed by your core values, you can bring harmony to your life during this season of caregiving.

God of harmony, help me hear the melody you've composed for my life during this season. In Jesus's name, amen.

Reflection: Listen closely. What is your life's melody for this season? What principles guide you now as a caregiver? What choice do you need to make to live out that sacred melody?

77

THE TYRANNY OF THE URGENT

But the Lord said to her, "My dear Martha, you are worried and upset over all these details! There is only one thing worth being concerned about. Mary has discovered it, and it will not be taken away from her." —Luke 10:41–42 NLT

Mom had been having coughing fits that awakened her and me in the middle of the night. On one occasion, I slept in a little because we had been up through much of the night. I awakened later than usual to go to the bathroom and heard the recycling trucks outside.

I peeked outside and saw the trucks on the other side of the street, which let me know that the workers would handle the bins on our side shortly. *Yikes!* I thought. We had yet to move our recycling bin to the curb.

I shifted into overdrive, and the urgent voice inside my head shouted: *I've got to get the recycling out NOW!*

I rushed downstairs. My clamoring must have awakened my husband. I yelled to him from the steps, "The recycling truck is coming!" with the same urgency as Paul Revere bellowing out the warning to the colonial revolutionaries: "The British are coming!"

I was having a Martha moment and had gotten caught up in what essayist Charles E. Hummel called the "tyranny of the urgent."[9] Living our lives in a way where everything is urgent can become oppressive.

In his book *The 7 Habits of Highly Effective People*, Stephen Covey coaches us to distinguish between what's important and what is urgent. We can plan for important things so they don't become urgent and cause us to go into overdrive, raising our adrenaline and creating conditions that ultimately are unhealthy for our overall well-being. And even when our plans fail, we must not allow failed plans to become a crisis in our heads.

Caring well for ourselves and our loved ones is important, and so is caring for our home environment. We plan for those important tasks. But sometimes, we forget. My husband forgot to take the recycling out the night before. Once I realized it, those bins still did not need to become an urgent matter. We had time to get them out before the trucks came to our side of the street. Later, I even asked myself if it would have been the end of the world if we had missed the truck. We could develop a Plan B and place new recycling items in the garage until the next pickup.

Too often, we turn important tasks into urgent ones, not because the priority of the task changes but because, in our hyper-busy culture, we've become wired for urgency. Urgency has become a mindset for too many of us, and we must settle down and rearrange our thinking.

Though everything seems urgent, we must focus on what is essential: caring well from a place of wholeness and wellness.

Dear God of liberation, free me from the tyranny of the urgent. In Jesus's name, amen.

Reflection: Think about how you've become wired for urgency. What can you do differently? How can you establish a healthy method of completing important tasks?

78

WORKING TOGETHER IN LOVE

Is there any encouragement from belonging
to Christ? Any comfort from his love?
Any fellowship together in the Spirit? Are
your hearts tender and compassionate?
Then make me truly happy by agreeing
wholeheartedly with each other, loving one
another, and working together with one mind
and purpose. —Philippians 2:1–2 NLT

My husband Carl and I married in our fifties, with our octogenarian parents bearing witness. A few years later, we were to become caregivers for all three of them, first for my mother and then for his parents, who were in their nineties. Though we were partners in marriage and ministry, some of the best lessons in working together came to us while caregiving for our respective parents.

It was a given that one of us would lead and the other support. Caregiving is not the time to bump heads over titles and who's in charge. When we brought my mom into our home, I took the lead in her caregiving as she was my mom. My siblings and I strategized her medical and financial needs, and I served as the on-the-ground caregiver. I coordinated her medical care, managed her meds and meals, and coordinated her caregiving assistance.

Carl provided excellent support. We had always shared

cooking, and we continued that. When I had an appointment and the caregiver was unavailable, Carl sat with Mom and kept her company or worked in his home office, letting her know he was nearby. He lavishly provided me with moral support and encouragement.

Carl's father was periodically hospitalized during our season of caring for Mom. Of course, Carl was the lead on attending to his dad. Shortly after Mom passed, Carl's father's health challenges increased, leading to multiple hospitalizations and time in skilled nursing facilities. Carl and his sisters coordinated their parents' care, and I provided support.

Caregiving is often a family affair. Too often, family members are spread out and live in different cities. Still, we can hopefully find a way to work together to provide the needed care.

The apostle Paul wrote such encouraging, uplifting words to the church family in Philippi. He emphasized most strongly their working together with one mind and purpose: "Don't be selfish; don't try to impress others. Be humble, thinking of others as better than yourselves. Don't look out only for your own interests, but take an interest in others, too" (Philippians 2:3–4 NLT).

At the heart of caregiving is the spirit of harmony, unity, and being of one accord. Caregiving does not happen in isolation or a vacuum. Regardless of family dynamics, caregiving is a family affair where all family members play a role.

God of families and fellowship, unite us in love
to provide the care needed for our loved ones
and ourselves. In Jesus's name, amen.

Reflection: Think about the ways your family supports your caregiving. Give thanks for that support. For family members who don't provide support, please find a way to forgive them.

79

LEARN TO BE CONTENT

I have learned to be content in any
circumstance. —Philippians 4:11 NET

Caregiving entails making many sacrifices. Sometimes the circumstances of our loved one's care create many needs, including financial ones. The additional financial demands can strain the budget and call for lifestyle changes.

Though I was blessed to be working from home then, I've spoken to many caregivers who had to quit their jobs to provide the care their loved ones needed. For some, suspending their career, even for a season, increased household budget stress. For others who had to remain employed, caregiving and working created a different type of hardship.

There are extreme ups and downs in caregiving. If we are not careful, these fluctuating circumstances can send us into flux. However, our inner state cannot be so tied to outward circumstances that we allow the situation to steal our peace. I believe that is what Paul conveyed to the Philippian church. Writing from a Roman prison, the apostle sent his letter to express thanks for their giving generously to his ministry. He starts out appealing to their continued unity. Along the way, he reveals the hardships he experienced in ministry, making their gift even more significant.

Recognizing that the believers had their own hardships, he encouraged them not to let their situations make them overly anxious. He encouraged them to experience the peace of God that comes through "prayer and petition with thanksgiving" (Philippians 4:6 NET). His prayer was that the "God of peace" would be with them (v. 9 NET).

Paul could write about such peace because he had been through extreme ups and downs himself and learned that he could be content in any circumstance. He emphasized his ability to allow "Christ's power to sustain in difficulty and scarcity, and to enhance the enjoyment of abundance."[10] Being content protected his peace.

Contemporary psychologists reinforce the relationship between contentment and peace: "Contentment means to be happy with what you have, who you are, and where you are. It is respecting the reality of the present. . . . Contentment brings peace of mind and positivity that can facilitate growth."[11] As caregivers, we must develop a contentment mindset that allows us to learn from situations without becoming so frustrated that we lose our peace.

Circumstances do not have to throw us into an emotional tailspin. We can handle both favorable and challenging circumstances because of Christ's all-sufficiency.

God of peace who sustains me, help me to be
content in every circumstance, knowing that
you are sufficient. In Jesus's name, amen.

Reflection: Contentment is about accepting who you are and where you are in this season of caregiving. Take some time to pray about your caregiving circumstances. If need be, ask God what is necessary to restore your peace.

80

PROTECT YOUR ENERGY

To this end I strenuously contend with
all the energy Christ so powerfully
works in me. —Colossians 1:29

Early on, I learned caregiving could be emotionally draining if I wasn't careful. A dear friend and clinical psychologist, Dr. Patricia Jones-Blessman, wrote a blog for the Caregiver's Corner that significantly shifted my perspective on how I provided caregiving.

She wrote this gem that stopped me in my tracks. I created a quote image, posted it on social media, and hung a flyer on the wall in my office to remind me of this pithy treasure: "You only have a finite amount of energy to give! Be careful of who you share it with and protect your peace at all costs."[12]

The stress of giving can cause energy to drain and can sap us emotionally. Dr. Jones-Blessman helped me to accept the finite amount of energy I have. God enables us to generate and hold an internal amount of energy to be effective in what we do. We hold this power from God within very human vessels that must recharge.

Like the writer of the above passage, we work hard and strive for our goals with the energy God gives us. The word *energeia* in the Bible, from which we get the English word *energy*, usually refers to the "working of God"[13] in us humans. Though God's power and energy are unlimited, ours are not. We need to protect our outlay of energy, and we also need to recharge.

Dr. Jones-Blessman gave a strategic recommendation on how we might protect our energy. She writes, "Caregivers are typical 'givers' in general and they tend to attract people who 'take.' You can protect yourself from this by limiting your interactions with people who are looking to be cared for. This can mean both emotionally, financially, or otherwise."[14] She reminded me that I could not care for everyone during this season of caring for Mom, and that I could say no to other requests.

As caregivers, many of us see caring for others as part of our purpose and calling. Being clear on who you are called to care for in each season is a critical self-care strategy. We must recharge through rest and life-giving, sustaining relationships. And we must stop believing we are responsible to take care of everyone, especially at the expense of ourselves.

God of all power and energy, you've designed me to be a rechargeable energy source. Still, I must rest, renew, and limit what I give and to whom, based on your leading. In Jesus's name, amen.

Reflection: Consider the many ways you spend energy as you care for others. Next, develop your strategy for being intentional with your outlay of energy.

SECTION 9

ENVIRONMENTAL WELL-BEING

81

MAKE ROOM

My Father's house has many rooms; if that were
not so, would I have told you that I am going
there to prepare a place for you? —John 14:2

One of my favorite streaming shows was *9-1-1*. I discovered it during my caregiving season and would watch episodes in the late-night hours by myself while I decompressed from the day. The show starred one of my favorite actors, Angela Bassett. One of the storylines of the first couple of seasons centered on Abby, a 911 operator who cared for her aging mother, who had Alzheimer's disease.

Abby converted her dining room into her mother's bedroom. I felt so seen by that depiction, as we had converted our family room into Mom's living area. Mom could not easily climb stairs as her respiratory and ambulatory issues progressed. Our split-level, older-style home presented too many fall risks for her. Therefore, we made room for my mother where it was safer and more comfortable for her.

The room was spacious enough to hold a hospital bed, her reclining chair, a television, lamps, and an oxygen tank. I purchased a decorative wicker room divider to give her privacy and to section off a part of the room for me to safely arrange her meds. The bathroom on that level was about forty steps from her bed or chair, which was manageable for Mom with her walker.

She loved her living area. Our home had become hers. We placed a loveseat in the room so my husband and I could spend family time with her. We went to her room for dinner and watched movies with her for family night. We prayed there and just sat and talked at times.

We made room for her by preparing a place for her. This is the message Jesus used to console His disciples, too. He was preparing them for His departure while assuring them that He was preparing an eternal place for them in heaven. He was making room for them (and for us).

Creating an environment where the loved ones we are caring for feel that they belong is crucial. Most aging parents (and others) don't want to feel as though they're a burden. Their well-being and ours can hinge on the environment for care that we create.

Few of us can purchase new homes or even renovate our current homes in order to bring our loved ones to live with us. But we gladly make room for them in our hearts, and in whatever ways we can, in our homes.

God, whose heavenly home is filled with many rooms, thank you for making space for us just as we make space for caring. In Jesus's name, amen.

Reflection: Take a moment to survey your home environment. Given the constraints you must work within, assess whether it is an optimal caring environment for you and your loved one. If you find the need for changes, please begin to make the adjustments—for your sake and that of your loved one.

82

CREATE THE ENVIRONMENT

The LORD God took the human and settled
him in the garden of Eden to farm it and
to take care of it. —Genesis 2:15 CEB

Perhaps Genesis 2:15 gives us the first instance of caregiving in the Bible—that of Adam, the first human, caring for the garden. The Lord God created a home for the first
humans in an idyllic place called Eden. It was beautiful and
filled with every type of vegetation the first humans needed
for sustenance. God provided this place for humans to thrive
and this gives us insight into the integral connection between
our environment and well-being.

The place and space where we care for our loved ones and
ourselves, and the caring atmosphere we help create, are just as
critical to our well-being. Our spaces (home, outdoors, work,
and the like) have a "direct impact on [our] state of mind, emotional well-being, and productivity."[1]

Environmental well-being is the wellness that emerges from
our living spaces and care. It can also include other settings in
which we exist: our outdoor spaces, indoor spaces, and work-
spaces. It's about how we intentionally create an atmosphere
that enhances our well-being. Environmental wellness is about
how our external environment can positively affect our internal
mindset.

For instance, some of us cherish light-filled rooms over

darkened rooms; we may feel the light clarifies our thinking and makes us happier. Cluttered spaces disrupt my thinking (as you will see in Devotion #84). As caregivers, our well-being is enhanced by creating spaces for ourselves to just be and where we can unwind in our own way (see Devotion #88).

Caregiving duties can be so time-consuming that we don't want to think about organizing or decorating our spaces. But little things can create a sense of calm amidst the sometimes chaotic caregiving processes. Turning on soft music to allow favorite tunes to stream through the air can lighten the mood. Bringing in flowers provides a fragrant reminder of God's creation, of which we are a part.

We each have the power to create a caring environment that can help us care for our loved ones and ourselves with more intentionality. We can use our imaginations to lighten the rigors of caregiving and create spaces that can be good for our well-being.

God of creation, fill my caregiving spaces with light and love. Please show me how to cultivate peace around me that enhances peace within me. In Jesus's name, amen.

Reflection: Take some time to prepare a list of items you can use to bring a little joy to your life.

83

THE POWER OF FLOWERS

Even the wilderness and desert will be glad
in those days. The wasteland will rejoice and
blossom with spring crocuses. Yes, there will be
an abundance of flowers and singing and joy! The
deserts will become as green as the mountains of
Lebanon, as lovely as Mount Carmel or the plain
of Sharon. There the LORD will display his glory,
the splendor of our God. —Isaiah 35:1–2 NLT

I started a flower garden during year two of the COVID-19 pandemic. Gardening became a time of quiet reflection as I dug into the soil, planted bushes and bulbs, and added protective layers of mulch to each flower group. Years prior, a church member had planted a beautiful peony plant for me in our backyard. I hadn't done much in previous years to care for it, but during the pandemic, I began to tend the plant with great care. That year, I also planted knock-out rose bushes, Asian lilies, and two butterfly bushes. I really dug into my new hobby!

Bright yellow daffodils bloomed in the early spring of the following year. I hadn't even planted those, but after tending to the soil around another set of flowers in the fall the year before, the previously dormant daffodil bulbs received the nourishment they needed to sprout up, to my great surprise and delight.

What started as a wilderness season for me and so many others transformed into one of great beauty. My backyard blossomed with an abundance of flowers. In the spring, summer, and early fall, my garden enabled me to keep our home, especially Mom's living space, stocked with fragrant, fresh-cut flowers.

When she was hospitalized, I brought to her room a vase full of round, plush peonies in the spring. Even the nurses marveled at the white pom-pom–like blooms. When she was released to rehab, I brought fresh-cut red roses each week. And then, the following spring, as she was nestled safely in our home, I brought a vase full of those dazzling yellow daffodils and set it on the mantle for her to enjoy. The look of awe on her face was priceless.

The prophet Isaiah used blossoming flowers and green vegetation to describe a time of hope and renewal for God's people. Even though they were experiencing tough times, God had a plan and used the prophet to provide a picture of hope and God's splendor.

Flowers remind us of renewal. They elicit hope within us. Flowers beautify our environment and perfume the air with calming fragrances. What started as pandemic therapy became a source of beauty, joy, and delight for my mom and me. Those flowers enhanced my well-being. Gardening became a time of self-care for me, and the flowers from the garden became objects of admiration for my mom and me.

Perhaps you don't have a garden and may not even be prone to starting one. But consider how flowers may beautify your environment and enhance your well-being.

Dear God, thank you for manifesting your splendor and glory in flowers. They speak of your abundance and remind us that just as you bring forth flowers, you also care for us. In Jesus's name, amen.

Reflection: What flower symbolizes hope for you? Consider getting those flowers to brighten up your space.

84

GRACE FOR THE PERFECTIONIST

May the grace of the Lord Jesus Christ be
with your spirit. —Philippians 4:23 NLT

Author Anne Lamott once wrote, "In the theological sense,"
grace is that "force that infuses our lives and keeps letting
us off the hook."[2] In managing caregiving and the rest of my
life, I needed the grace to let myself off my perfectionism hook.

Let's talk about perfectionism as caregivers. For any of us who
struggle with perfectionistic tendencies, trying to manage caregiving tasks perfectly will cause us added anxiety and stress. Before you say you are not a perfectionist, researcher Brené Brown
has found that "perfectionism exists along a continuum. We all
have some perfectionistic tendencies."[3] She explains that perfectionism peeks out when one is feeling vulnerable. For some
of us, perfectionism can be chronic and ongoing.

I am a recovering perfectionist and have learned the difference between striving for perfection and working in excellence to achieve goals in my professional and personal life.
Yet I found that running a business and caregiving during the
pandemic left me vulnerable and easy prey for perfectionism
to creep back into my mindset.

Here's an example of what it looked like in the early days of
caregiving for me: I meticulously organized and color-coded
all the client files in my home office so that I could find what
I needed for client calls at a glance.

As the demands of caregiving increased, I began to rely upon electronic bill paying and client invoicing. I had less time to perfectly file the hardcopy bills, client invoices, and other documents. I began to stack them up next to my computer monitor.

What started as a stressful feeling from seeing that paper pile up eventually settled into being OK. I had to extend grace to myself and to accept that some things wouldn't look as neat as they once did. I came to realize that the piles did not diminish who I was. I didn't need to be embarrassed because my office was perpetually messy. I thanked God for the blur option on video conferencing platforms and kept meetings moving.

I had to let go of the image of the perfect business professional as measured by her perfect office, because I was a woman caring for her aging mother while managing client calls during a pandemic. Grace shows up to guide us through our being disappointed with ourselves for not managing life perfectly and settles us firmly in God's perfect love and acceptance.

Dear perfect God, thank you for filling in the gaps of my imperfections. In Jesus's name, amen.

Reflection: On the continuum of perfectionism, where do you fall? How can you recognize perfectionism when it shows itself? What perfect image do you need to let go of in order to be OK with your imperfections?

85

CLEAR THE CLUTTER

For God is not a God of disorder but of
peace. —1 Corinthians 14:33 NLT

Long before we each became caregivers to our mother, my
brother and I shared a home when we each relocated to
the Chicago area. We had a mantra, "A place for everything,
and everything in its place." We tried to live by that, but because of our busy schedules, things would periodically pile up.
Then my brother would admonish, "It's time to clear the clutter." For both of us, that meant getting organized in our environment and our minds!

Clutter is not the same thing as having a dirty or unsafe environment. A cluttered space or room is disorderly or messy.
It prohibits our ability to be effective and efficient in those
spaces.

I maintained the habit of being orderly and decluttered
when caring for Mom. Her care assistant, Denise, and I organized her clothes. I bought special hangers for her clothes, and
we arranged her closet by type of garment. This made it easier
for us to identify clothing each morning (and, of course, Denise always asked Mom what she wanted to wear and would
bring a few outfits out so that Mom could choose).

We organized her personal-care supplies on shelves and in
drawers designated just for them. I kept a list of Mom's medi-
cations on a credenza reserved for her prescriptions. I lined
up each prescription bottle in order, like little toy soldiers
ready for battle. This organization made it easier for me to

fill her pill case, which was organized by days of the week and included spaces for morning, afternoon, evening, and night. Being organized helped relieve the stress of managing meds and gave me peace that I hadn't missed anything.

I learned that being disorganized can cause stress. We become stretched looking for things that should be accessible or at our fingertips. We get frustrated when we can't find an item we need immediately. Being disorganized, however, can also be a symptom of stress. Some of us may get so overwhelmed with the demands of caregiving that we let things pile up (as I did in my home office). In those cases, we become more stressed when we are not organized, which then causes us to become more disorganized and more stressed. Thus, the vicious cycle continues.

We can break that cycle of stressed-induced disorganization. Getting and staying organized starts with the intention to organize our environment. It can start with committing to organize each part of our living environment and planning the time to do it.

Having a place for the things in our lives, including the things we need for caregiving, is vital to our environmental order and well-being.

God of order, just as your Spirit hovered over the chaos at creation, hover over me and help me to clear the clutter in my life. In Jesus's name, amen.

Reflection: It can feel overwhelming to reorganize your entire life or home at once. Identify a top priority, schedule the work, and ask for help. Where might be an excellent place to start clearing the clutter in your caregiving life?

86

THE TIME TO ORGANIZE

A time to search and a time to quit
searching. A time to keep and a time to
throw away. —Ecclesiastes 3:6 NLT

When we frequently cannot keep track of the personal items in our home, such as our keys, wallets, purses, personal papers, or even small objects such as paper clips or hairpins, chances are it's time to get organized. Now keep in mind that all of us have the occasional moments when we can't find our glasses (when they are atop our head) or have experienced looking for our smartphone (while talking on that same phone).

Losing things or being unable to readily locate stuff in our environment because of clutter and messiness suggests that it's time to stop searching for those things and start organizing. It's time to decide what we need to keep and what we need to throw or give away.

When disorganization becomes a habit, it most likely affects all parts of our lives. We can find our finances disorganized, and now we must manage our loved one's finances as well. We may discover that we don't organize or plan our time well, so we don't feel we have accomplished much at the end of the day.

So, the first thing we need to do in getting organized is to take time to become still and seek help and guidance through prayer. Bringing organization to our spiritual lives will help us develop a strategy for organizing other parts of our lives.

Next, we need to define what organization means to us

and what it may need to look like, given our different care-giving situations. We must release ourselves from comparing our homes to those on social media or in magazines.

Then, we must start one place at a time, one day at a time. We can get overwhelmed if we take on too much at any given time. Instead, identifying which room, closet, or space we need to start with will keep us from thinking the task of organizing is too large.

We need to create a rule of thumb for keeping and discarding items. Think about what we need to keep in terms of things necessary for running our homes, that bring delight to our family, and that are still useful. Think about the things we need to discard that have not been used in years, no longer serve a purpose, and are taking up space and adding to the clutter. We each need to develop guidelines for what works for us. Staying organized is a healthy practice for maintaining our well-being as caregivers.

God of strategic timing, thank you for sensitizing me to the time to get organized. I see your wisdom in planning and ask now for your grace in making it happen. In Jesus's name, amen.

Reflection: Carve out some quiet time to organize your thoughts around what needs to be done first, and set a schedule for starting.

87

LET IT GO

Do not remember the former things, nor
consider the things of old. —Isaiah 43:18 NKJV

Organizing our spaces for caregiving can be challenging if
we have difficulty letting go. When we find that our areas
have become cluttered, if we look closely at the things that
have piled up, we find that most of them are things from our
past that we've allowed to accumulate. Of course, there also are
mementos and pictures from our past that help us memorial-
ize our family heritage or capture memories of past events.

Yet some things from the past that we're still attached to
may hold us to an old identity that we need to discard and
leave behind. We've grown, but our things don't represent that
growth.

Today's Scripture passage admonishes us to forget the former things. The prophet Isaiah was writing to the people of
God who were in bondage, and he was preparing them for their
eventual release. He described God's plan to release them from
bondage as being the "new thing" God was doing for them.

For God's people, not remembering the past did not mean
forgetting what God had done and brought them through (see
Isaiah 46:9). Instead, it meant not letting past struggles and
identity as a nation occupy their minds so that they missed
what was happening now.

We can allow the past to occupy our minds so that we have
difficulty letting go of things, even though they serve no purpose for our present or where God is taking us. Letting go

takes the courage to release ourselves from our past, even as God is preparing us for a hope-filled future.

The first step in letting go of the things that have piled up in our lives is to ask ourselves what purpose these things serve for who we are today. We must resist creating a future mythic purpose for those things. We can tell ourselves stories about the future and justify holding on to past things . . . just in case we need them. In many cases, the items we have allowed to pile up are less about the things themselves but about our attachment to the things and to a perception of ourselves that no longer is true.

As we choose to let go, we can identify places to discard items. We can donate fashionable clothes that no longer fit to local family shelters. We can donate old household items to families from church. Many of us recognize the costs we invested in these items, but we don't need to remain attached to that investment. Our letting go can be the first step in blessing someone else.

Dear God, I will never forget to thank you for graciously getting me to this place. As I let go of an unhealthy attachment to the past, I celebrate my present, and I trust you for my future. In Jesus's name, amen.

Reflection: What's the first step you need to take to let go of old items keeping your space cluttered?

88

DON'T LET DISTRACTIONS DISTRACT YOU

> But Martha was distracted by the big dinner
> she was preparing. She came to Jesus and said,
> "Lord, doesn't it seem unfair to you that my
> sister just sits here while I do all the work? Tell
> her to come and help me." —Luke 10:40 NLT

Every day, we face constant stimuli that competes for our attention. We have multiple alerts on multiple devices: "Stand up for 1 min"; "Motion has been detected at your front door." Dings and rings sing out to us, beckoning us to do something. And these interruptions become distractions as they divert our attention from our tasks.

The neighborhood ring alert goes off while we're concentrating on organizing meds. The evening newscaster interrupts our dinner prep, reporting on a series of carjackings in our neighborhood. The telemarketing call comes in just as we are getting our loved one ready for bed.

No wonder we, like Martha, have become worried and troubled about many things. These things cause us to become annoyed, impatient, and sometimes just downright irritated. We go into an internal tizzy when we allow demands and disruptions to get inside of us and distract us from the main thing, which is caring well for ourselves and our loved ones.

Pastor Rich Villodas in *The Deeply Formed Life* reminds us that "our distractions, whether in the moment of silent prayer or in the moment of steady demands, do not need to ruin our lives with God."[4] Pastor Villodas also reminds us that our irritation with the interruption is telling. "Like Martha, Jesus had plenty of moments of nonstop activity, yet he remained anchored in attentive presence with His Father. Perhaps the issue with Martha is not her busyness but her lack of inner attentiveness."[5] In other words, when we stay centered in our hearts and attitudes, we won't become so irritated by the disruptions as we accept that they are part of the busy caregiving life. Instead, the distractions can become an invitation to take a deep breath, invite the Spirit to refocus us, and return to what we were doing.

Too often, we allow distractions to divert our attention. Instead of noting it and remaining focused on our primary task, we turn our attention to the ding, the ring. Caring well entails learning to remain centered in our heart and soul. To cultivate that center of peace, we need to put our devices on Do Not Disturb during certain hours to minimize disruptions.

But distractions will invariably come. The key is to cultivate the habit of returning to our internal center, where the well of the Spirit flows.

Dear God of peace, center me in your love. I accept that there will be distractions, but they don't have to disrupt my peace. In Jesus's name, amen.

Reflection: Think of a word or phrase you can use to bring you back to focus. Try using this word or phrase the next time a distraction threatens to disrupt your peace.

89

MY SPACE

But you, when you pray, go into your room,
and when you have shut your door, pray
to your Father who is in the secret place;
and your Father who sees in secret will
reward you openly. —Matthew 6:6 NKJV

Jesus taught prayer practices to His followers that were contrary to the religious leaders who "loved to pray standing in the synagogues and on the corner of streets that they may be seen by" people (Matthew 6:5). Instead, Jesus taught His followers to go into their rooms, shut the door, and talk to God.

In addition to anchoring our prayer lives in unpretentious, unostentatious practice, Jesus's teaching on prayer also reinforces the importance of having one's own space to go and be alone with the Lord.

My space was our reading room. We dedicated one bedroom in our home for me to read and pray. Long before Mom came to live with us, I'd retreat to this room to pray when awakened at three or four in the morning. Or I'd sit for hours on a free Saturday reading another novel. Simply furnished with a sofa that converted to a bed (to become sleeping quarters for guests), a bookcase full of books, a table and lamp, and an Akan throne I bought in Ghana, that was my space.

Once I became a caregiver, it was to this space that I'd retreat each night around eleven p.m., after a long day of work and caregiving. Mom was nestled snugly in bed, watching her Western shows. My husband had gone to bed. I'd go into my space and close the door. I'd thank God for another day. Then, I'd put earbuds in and tune into one of my favorite streaming services to watch another episode of some show. The shows became great ways for me to unwind in my space at the end of the day.

Having our own space provides a place where we can just be. They are places where we can do what we need to care for ourselves. A basement or guest-bedroom workout area can become a "my space." We can create a temporary "my space" in the bathroom as we close the door, fill the tub with water and fragrant bath salts or oil, light candles, and dip into our private spa.

In our spaces, we can attend to ourselves. We pamper ourselves for a few moments a day or at some time during the week, with no apologies, no guilt.

Dear God, who sees and hears us, thank you for showing up in my space and letting me be me. In Jesus's name, amen.

Reflection: If you haven't already done so, identify a "my space" in your home. Consider how you can set aside regular time to spend in that place.

90

FILL THE ROOM WITH AROMA

Oil and perfume make the heart glad; so
does the sweetness of a friend's counsel that
comes from the heart. —Proverbs 27:9 AMP

Nothing is more refreshing than the fragrance of eucalyptus oil wafting through my house. I pour a few drops into my water-filled diffuser and breathe in, allowing the aroma to settle my soul. I pour eucalyptus bath salt into a tub of hot water and ease in to soak and relax my mind. Eucalyptus oil is said to have a clearing and invigorating effect.

Scents signal the part of the brain that controls memory and emotions. Certain fragrances elicit positive emotions and "have been proven to lower stress levels," "improve overall mental outlook," and can "significantly promote stress reduction and improve mood."[6]

Fragrances and oils are ancient, and scholars have found evidence of their use in many cultures—no wonder the biblical proverb likens fragrant oils and perfumes to the sweetness of friends. Though fragrances and oils are very ancient, the contemporary benefits for our well-being belong to the science of aromatherapy. Aromatherapy uses essential oils to promote "the health of the body, mind, and spirit."[7]

There are many ways to incorporate aromatherapy into your self-care routine. We can research to learn more about the benefits of different essential oils that might work for us.

There are numerous products to use with your fragrant oils. Some examples include: "diffusers, aromatic spritzers, inhalers, bathing salts, body oils, creams, or lotions for massage or topical application, facial steamers, hot and cold compresses, and clay masks."[8] We can gravitate to the ones that best fit into our homes, space, and lifestyle.

Strategically placing aroma products in home offices, bedrooms, and living rooms can be a good reminder for us as caregivers that caring for ourselves is a part of caregiving. Of course, we must remember to pay attention to how different fragrances affect our loved ones and minimize unhealthy reactions. As caregivers, we might want to limit our aromatherapy to our healing self-care space.

Oils and fragrances can help create a healing, calming presence in our homes or an uplifting, energizing feel. Using aromatherapy allows us to create an environment of wellness that can enhance our overall well-being.

Dear God, thank you for the sweetness of elements from your good creation that enhance our well-being. In Jesus's name, amen.

Reflection: Take some time to experiment with oils and other fragrances, taking note of their effects on your mood.

ACKNOWLEDGMENTS

Assuming the role of caregiver initiates each of us into a distinct and ever-expanding group. Few understand the gravity of caregiving until they enter this league. I pray this book of devotions is as much of a blessing to each of you as it has been for me in reflecting, recalling, and writing. The journey has been healing. May these devotions become foundational to your ongoing self-care.

It feels only fitting to write these acknowledgments on the first anniversary of Mom's passing. Without my mother, Marjorie Porter, there'd be no *Caring Well* devotional book. I learned much about caring for her and myself during that season.

I am grateful to my husband, Dr. Carl E. King Sr., whom Mom affectionately called "Pastor." He welcomed my mother into our home and loved her graciously. And she loved him. He was the steady influence in our house, an ear for me, arms that held me, and my partner in care. My fondest memories of that season are of our family times, including shared meals, watching movies, and our nightly evening worship and prayer time. That was restorative for all of us.

When Mom came to live with us, I periodically posted about our experiences on my Facebook page. I was amazed at the number of people who identified with those posts. Countless people would respond that they needed the post's message as they were also caring for a loved one. Others would remark that they had previously cared for their loved one and were witnesses that I would likewise get through this season. I never realized how many people in my social media and faith communities were or had been caregivers. It seems that caregiving is often done in silence or privately.

Because of those responses, I felt led by the Holy Spirit to launch a Caregivers blog. I invited people in my community to share their stories of caregiving. I am thankful that Katara Washington Patton, executive editor for VOICES from Our Daily Bread Publishing, saw the blog and invited me to write a proposal for a self-care devotional book for caregivers. I immediately saw that as a marvelous and much-needed resource for caregivers. Katara, you've been a joy and inspiration to work with.

I am incredibly thankful for my literary agent, Jevon Bolden. Jevon is supportive and inspiring. I am especially grateful to be a part of the Embolden Media Group.

I must give a special thanks to Denise Evans, Relief Care @ Home Caregiving Service's president, and her team of caregivers. We became more than a team; we became family. Their presence and assistance were crucial to my care strategy, enabling me to continue to work, exercise, run errands, and have some "me time." And I am forever grateful for Dan Franklin and his team at Essential Home Health for providing the medical professionals we needed for Mom's care.

I give special thanks to my brother Joe, sister-in-love Tamara, sister Jocelyn, and brother-in-love Bruce. Moving Mom out of state—away from my siblings and their families during a pandemic—was difficult for everyone. Yet they provided loving support that helped me do what I needed to do. Their calls and family visits brought such joy to Mom—and me.

I must give a special acknowledgment to Mom's grandchildren, Daniel, Channing, Kristen, Kiara, Kiandria, and Taylor. They loved Grandma and showed it! Their regular calls and video chats delighted Mom, and seeing their closeness brought joy to me too. And you should have seen her face light up when they could travel to Illinois to visit her.

I am grateful for cousins who made a point to come into town and spend time with Mom: Heather, Brian, Adell, Mike, Dawn, Larraine, and Sherrice (Reesie). Your visits brought joy to Mom and to me.

I thank God for Dr. Yolanda Peppers, who, having lost her own mother a few years prior, adopted Mom as hers and regularly checked in. On two occasions, my husband and I needed to take overnight trips, and we entrusted Mom to Yolanda for overnight care. As she would say, "Bless the King!" Special thanks go to my sister in pastoral ministry, Evang. Ivory Nuckolls, her sister Babs, and their mother whom I affectionately call Mom Barb Lee. They regularly called to check on Mom and me and made sure they celebrated her birthdays.

Finally, two dear friends living out of state made a point to come into town and check on Mom and me: Dr. Debbye Turner Bell and Dr. Brenda Salter-McNeil. I will forever be grateful for that sisterhood.

As I wrote in these pages, I realized that caregiving and writing about caregiving take a village. I am grateful for my village!

NOTES

Section 1: Enhancing Spiritual Well-Being

1. Suzette Caldwell, *Praying to Change Your Life: A Guide to Productive Prayer* (Shippensburg, PA: Destiny Image Publishers, 2009), 83.

2. Caldwell, *Praying to Change Your Life*, 85–86.

Section 2: Drawing from the Culture

1. Barry Jr. Jacobs, "Community and Culture Help Black Caregivers Cope with the Challenges of Family Caregiving." AARP, February 9, 2021, https://www.aarp.org/caregiving/basics/info-2021/african -american-caregivers-cope-better.html (accessed April 1, 2024).

2. Jacobs, "Community and Culture Help Black Caregivers."

3. "How Systemic Racism and a Global Pandemic Impacts Caregivers of Color," *California Caregiver* blog, https://www. caregivercalifornia.org/2021/07/08/how-systemic-racism-and-a-global-pandemic-impacts-caregivers-of-color/ (accessed April 1, 2024).

4. "Lift Every Voice and Sing," NAACP website, https://naacp.org /find-resources/history-explained/lift-every-voice-and-sing (accessed April 1, 2024).

5. *Online Etymology Dictionary*, see "legacy," https://www.etymonline .com/search?q=legacy (accessed April 3, 2024).

6. "You Can't Make Me Doubt Him," Hymnary.org, c.1900, https:// hymnary.org/text/you_cant_make_me_doubt_him (accessed April 3, 2024).

7. *Strong's Exhaustive Concordance of the Bible* (Peabody, MA: Hendrickson Publishers, 2007), 1621.

8. For background information, see Michael Hawn, "*Siyahamba, South African Freedom Song,*" *The Chorister*, December 1999, https://www.choristersguild.org/userfiles/MA_TeachResources/Siyahamba.pdf (accessed April 3, 2024).

9. Janelle Harris Dixon, "Why the Black National Anthem Is Lifting Every Voice to Sing," *Smithsonian Magazine*, August 10, 2020, https://www.smithsonianmag.com/smithsonian-institution/why-black-national-anthem-lifting-every-voice-sing-180975519/ (accessed April 1, 2024).

10. "Lift Every Voice."

11. Leo Newhouse, "Is Crying Good For You?" *Harvard Health Blog*, March 1, 2021, https://www.health.harvard.edu/blog/is-crying-good-for-you-2021030122020 (accessed April 1, 2024).

12. Newhouse, "Is Crying Good."

13. "Lift Every Voice."

14. "Black Joy," Dictionary.com, January 28, 2022, https://www.dictionary.com/e/historical-current-events/black-joy/ (accessed April 3, 2024).

15. Elaine Nichols, "Black Joy: Resistence, Resilience and Reclamation," Smithonian, https://nmaahc.si.edu/explore/stories/black-joy-resistance-resilience-and-reclamation (accessed April 1, 2024).

16. Nichols, "Black Joy."

17. Noelle Toumy Reetz, "Self-Care as an Act of Resistance," *Georgia State University Research Magazine*, https://news.gsu.edu/research-magazine/self-care-black-women-yoga (accessed April 1, 2024).

Section 3: Personal Well-Being

1. Henri Nouwen, *Spiritual Direction: Wisdom for the Long Walk of Faith* (New York: HarperCollins, 2006), 27.

2. Nouwen, *Spiritual Direction*, 28.

3. James Strong, *The Exhaustive Concordance of the Bible: Showing Every Word of the Text of the Common English Version of the Canonical Books,* (Nashville: Abingdon, 1983), 59.

4. Robert A. Stein, *Luke: An Exegetical and Theological Exposition of Holy Scripture* (Nashville: B & H Publishing Group, 1993), 347.

5. Marianne Schnall, "An Interview with Maya Angelou," *Psychology Today*, February 17, 2009. https://www.psychologytoday.com/us /blog/the-guest-room/200902/interview-maya-angelou (accessed April 1, 2024).

6. Sara Kettler, "Maya Angelou: The Meaning Behind Her Poem, 'Still I Rise,'" updated January 29, 2021, https://www.biography .com/authors-writers/maya-angelou-still-i-rise (accessed April 1, 2024).

7. Jack Hayford, editor, *NIV, New Spirit-Filled Life Bible: Kingdom Equipping through the Power of the Word* (Nashville: Thomas Nelson, 2014), 1669.

Section 4: Relational Well-Being

1. Taylor Bennett, "8 Keys to Healthy Relationships, According to Mental Health Professionals," *Thriveworks*, https://thriveworks .com/blog/8-keys-healthy-relationships-mental-health -professionals/ (accessed April 1, 2024).

2. Richard C. Meyer, *One Anothering: Biblical Building Block for Small Groups*, vol. 1 (Minneapolis, MN: Augsburg Books, 2004).

3. Jeffrey Kranz, "All the 'one another' commands in the NT," overviewbible.com, March 9, 2014, https://overviewbible.com/one -another-infographic/ (accessed April 2, 2024).

4. Jeanne Porter King. This devotion is excerpted from a blog post published on January 17, 2023, on *Caregiver Corner*. Used by permission. https://www.drjeanneporterking.com/celebrating-one -year-of-caregivers-corner-3-lessons-from-year-one/ (accessed April 1, 2024).

5. "What Exactly Is a Holy Kiss?" Gotquestions.org, https://www .gotquestions.org/holy-kiss.html (accessed April 1, 2024).

6. "A Holy Kiss—What Is It?" *Compelling Truth*, compellingtruth .org, https://www.compellingtruth.org/holy-kiss.html (accessed April 1, 2024).

7. Jeanne Porter King, *Leading Well: A Black Woman's Guide to Wholistic, Barrier-Breaking Leadership* (Grand Rapids, MI: Baker Books, 2023), 36.

8. Henry Cloud and John Townsend, *Boundaries Updated and Expanded Edition: When to Say Yes, How to Say No to Take Control of Your Life* (Grand Rapids, MI: Zondervan, 2017), 27.

Section 5: Mental and Intellectual Well-Being

1. Daphne M. Davis and Jeffrey A. Hayes, "What Are the Benefits of Mindfulness?," *Monitor on Psychology*, 43, no. 7 (July/August 2012): 64, https://www.apa.org/monitor/2012/07-08/ce-corner (accessed April 1, 2024).

2. Jeanne Porter King, *Leading Well: A Black Woman's Guide to Wholistic, Barrier-Breaking Leadership* (Grand Rapids, MI: Baker Books, 2023), 21.

3. Dave Anderson, Chris Martin, and Emily Quirk, "Bend but Don't Break: How Trees Survive Northern Winters," *Something Wild*, Forest Society, February 12, 2021, https://forestsociety.org /something-wild/bend-dont-break-how-trees-survive-northern -winters (accessed April 1, 2024).

4. Anderson, "Bend but Don't Break."

5. "Positive Thinking: Stop Negative Self-Talk to Reduce Stress," Mayo Clinic, https://www.mayoclinic.org/healthy-lifestyle/stress -management/in-depth/positive-thinking/art-20043950 (accessed April 1, 2024).

6. "Positive Thinking."

Section 6: Emotional Well-Being

1. Stephen R. Covey, *The 7 Habits of Highly Effective People*, electronic edition (New York: RosettaBooks LLC, 2009), 70.

2. Covey, *The 7 Habits*, 71.

3. Covey, *The 7 Habits*, 71.

4. "Word Wealth: Care," *New Spirit-Filled Life Bible* (Nashville: Thomas Nelson, 2002), 1769.

5. "Compassion Fatigue: Symptoms to Look For," medically reviewed by Smitha Bhandari WebMD, December 12, 2022, https:// www.webmd.com/mental-health/signs-compassion-fatigue (accessed April 3, 2024).

6. Brené Brown, *Atlas of the Heart: Mapping Meaningful Connection and the Language of Human Experience* (New York: Random House, 2021), 125.

7. "The Powerful Lesson Maya Angelou Taught Oprah," *Oprah Winfrey Network*, aired October 19, 2011, https://www.oprah.com /oprahs-lifeclass/the-powerful-lesson-maya-angelou-taught-oprah -video (accessed April 3, 2024).

8. Brown, *Atlas of the Heart*, 220.

9. Brown, *Atlas of the Heart*, 225.

Section 7: Physical Well-Being

1. Shani Saks, Reitze Rodseth, and Lynette Stewart, "Human Body Systems," OpenMD, https://openmd.com/guide/human-body-systems (accessed April 2, 2024).

2. "Physical Wellness Toolkit," National Institutes of Health, https://www.nih.gov/health-information/physical-wellness-toolkit (accessed April 2, 2024).

3. Carol Bradley Bursack, "Thirty Percent of Caregivers Die before the People They Care for Do," Caregiver Forum, AgingCare, October 2007, https://www.agingcare.com/discussions/thirty-percent-of-caregivers-die-before-the-people-they-care-for-do-97626.htm (accessed April 2, 2024).

4. "Gene Wilder's Widow on What It's Like to Care for Someone with Alzheimer's," *ABC News*, January 2, 2018, https://abcnews.go.com/Entertainment/gene-wilders-widow-care-alzheimers/story?id=52045475 (accessed April 3, 2024).

5. *Concise Oxford English Dictionary*, 10th ed. (2002), s.v. "sleep."

6. "Why Sleep Is Important," National Institutes of Health, last modified March 24, 2022, https://www.nhlbi.nih.gov/health/sleep/why-sleep-important (accessed April 3, 2024).

7. Joe Leech, "10 Reasons to Get More Sleep," Healthline, last modified April 25, 2023, https://www.healthline.com/nutrition/10-reasons-why-good-sleep-is-important (accessed April 3, 2024).

8. *New Spirit-Filled Life Bible*, (Nashville: Thomas Nelson, 2013), 637.

9. *New Spirit-Filled Life Bible*, 637.

10. Lawrence Robinson, Melinda Smith, and Jeanne Segal, "Laughter Is the Best Medicine," HelpGuide.org, last modified February 5, 2024, https://www.helpguide.org/articles/mental-health/laughter-is-the-best-medicine.htm (accessed April 3, 2024).

11. Ashley Zlatopolsky, "6 Unexpected Health Benefits of Walking," Real Simple, Dotdash Meredith, last modified June 12, 2023, https://www.realsimple.com/health/fitness-exercise/walking-benefits (accessed April 3, 2024).

12. Arlene Semeco, "The Top 10 Benefits of Regular Exercise," Healthline, last modified November 13, 2023 https://www.healthline.com/nutrition/10-benefits-of-exercise (accessed April 3, 2024).

13. "Relaxation Techniques: Breath Control Helps Quell Errant Stress Response," Harvard Health Publishing, July 6, 2020, https://www.health.harvard.edu/mind-and-mood/relaxation-techniques-breath-control-helps-quell-errant-stress-response (accessed April 3, 2024).

14. "Parasympathetic Nervous System (PSNS)," Cleveland Clinic, last modified June 6, 2022, https://my.clevelandclinic.org/health/body/23266-parasympathetic-nervous-system-psns (accessed April 3, 2024).

15. "Health Benefits of Eating Well," NHS inform, NHS 24, last modified January 4, 2023, https://www.nhsinform.scot/healthy-living/food-and-nutrition/eating-well/health-benefits-of-eating-well (accessed April 3, 2024).

16. "Health Benefits."

17. "Eating Well for Mental Health," Sutter Health, https://www.sutterhealth.org/health/nutrition/eating-well-for-mental-health (accessed April 3, 2024).

18. "Eating Well."

Section 8: Vocational Well-Being

1. Jennifer A. Kingson, "Even Your Boss Wants to Quit," Axios, June 22, 2022, https://www.axios.com/2022/06/22/ceo-csuite-burnout-pandemic-great-resignation (accessed April 3, 2024).

2. Nicholas Pearce, *The Purpose Path: A Guide to Pursuing Your Authentic Life's Work* (New York: St. Martin's Essentials, 2019), 223.

3. Lynn Friss-Feinberg and Laura Skufca, "Managing a Paid Job and Family Caregiving Is a Growing Reality," AARP, December 16, 2020, https://doi.org/10.26419/ppi.00103.024 (accessed April 3, 2024).

4. Parker Palmer, *Let Your Life Speak: Listening for the Voice of Vocation* (San Francisco: Jossey-Bass, 2000), 4.

5. Toni Alvarado, *Harmonize Your Life: A Journey Toward Self-Care* (self-pub. 2018), 14.

6. Alvarado, *Harmonize Your Life*, 14.

7. Alvarado, *Harmonize Your Life*, 14.

8. Dictionary.com, s.v. "harmony," https://www.dictionary.com/browse/harmony (accessed April 3, 2024).

9. Charles E. Hummel, *Tyranny of the Urgent,* rev. ed. (Downers Grove, IL: InterVarsity Press, 1994).

10. *New Spirit-Filled Life Bible*, (Nashville: Thomas Nelson, 2013), 1554.

11. Jacqueline Pearce, "The Essence of Contentment: How Acceptance Promotes Happiness," *The GoodTherapy Blog*, September 11, 2019, https://www.goodtherapy.org/blog/the-essence-of -contentment-how-acceptance-promotes-happiness-0911194 (accessed April 3, 2024).

12. Patricia Jones-Blessman, "Maintaining Emotional Strength," *Caregiver's Corner* (blog), March 16, 2022, https://www .drjeanneporterking.com/maintaining-emotional-strength (accessed April 3, 2024).

13. "Word Wealth: Working," *New Spirit-Filled Life Bible*, (Nashville: Thomas Nelson, 2013), 1673.

14. Jones-Blessman, "Maintaining Emotional Strength."

Section 9: Environmental Well-Being

1. Ben Mumme, "6 Ways to Enhance Your Environmental Wellness," Medium, April 14, 2021, https://medium.com/change-becomes -you/6-ways-to-enhance-your-environmental-wellness -2c915a374864 (accessed April 4, 2024).

2. Anne Lamott, *Traveling Mercies: Some Thoughts on Faith* (New York: Anchor Books, 1999), 139.

3. Brené Brown, *The Gifts of Imperfection: Let Go of Who You Think You're Supposed to Be and Embrace Who You Are* (Center City, MN: Hazelden, 2010), 58.

4. Rich Villodas, *The Deeply Formed Life: Five Transformative Values to Root Us in the Way of Jesus* (Colorado Springs: Waterbrook, 2020), 27–28.

5. Villodas, *The Deeply Formed Life*, 27.

6. "The Subtle Connection between Scent and Emotional Well-being," Air-Scent International, September 16, 2019, https://www .airscent.com/scent-and-emotional-well-being/ (accessed April 4, 2024).

7. Emily Cronkleton, "Aromatherapy Uses and Benefits," Healthline, last modified March 8, 2019, https://www.healthline.com/health /what-is-aromatherapy (accessed April 4, 2024).

8. Cronkleton, "Aromatherapy Uses and Benefits."

ABOUT THE AUTHOR

Dr. Jeanne Porter King is an author, consultant, pastor, and coach specializing in women's leadership and wellness. A trusted teacher and guide, she is passionate about empowering the whole woman. Dr. Porter King is the founder and president of TransPorter Group Inc., a consulting company that provides tools and resources for people to live, lead, and be well. She lives in Illinois with her husband, Pastor Carl E. King Sr., and she loves to read, bike, and tend to her garden.

PERMISSIONS

Scripture quotations, unless otherwise indicated, are taken from the Holy Bible, New International Version®, NIV®. Copyright © 1973, 1978, 1984, 2011 by Biblica, Inc.™ Used by permission of Zondervan. All rights reserved worldwide. www.zondervan.com.

Scripture quotations marked AMP are taken from the Amplified® Bible, Copyright © 2015 by The Lockman Foundation. Used by permission. lockman.org.

Scripture quotations marked CEB are taken from the COMMON ENGLISH BIBLE. © Copyright 2011 COMMON ENGLISH BIBLE. All rights reserved. Used by permission. (www.CommonEnglishBible.com).

Scripture quotations marked ERV are taken from the HOLY BIBLE: EASY-TO-READ VERSION © 2014 by Bible League International. Used by permission.

Scripture quotations marked MSG are taken from *The Message*, copyright © 1993, 2002, 2018 by Eugene H. Peterson. Used by permission of NavPress. All rights reserved. Represented by Tyndale House Publishers.

Spread the Word
by Doing One Thing.

- Give a copy of this book as a gift.
- Share the QR code link via your social media.
- Write a review of this book on your blog, favorite bookseller's website, or at ODB.org/store.
- Recommend this book to your church, small group, or book club.

Connect with us. 🇫 📷

Our Daily Bread Publishing
PO Box 3566, Grand Rapids, MI 49501, USA
Email: books@odb.org

See Us.

Hear Us.

Experience VOICES.

VOICES amplifies the strengths, struggles, and courageous faith of Black image bearers of God.

Podcasts, blogs, books, films, and more ...

Find out more at **experiencevoices.org**

Love God. Love Others.

with 🌾 Our Daily Bread.

Your gift changes lives.

Connect with us. 🇫 📷

Our Daily Bread Publishing
PO Box 3566, Grand Rapids, MI 49501, USA
Email: books@odb.org